Advanced Bass Tuition

Exercises and pieces practicing advanced techniques for Bass guitar

Written by Marcus Gee

Audio demonstrations available on Cd

Exercises with an audio demonstration are indicated by the Cd icon and a corresponding track number.

Advanced Bass Tuition copyright © 2014
Marcusgeebass.com

All pieces and exercises composed by Marcus Gee
Edited by Jacqui Gee and Adrian Hull
Book design and layout by Marcus Gee
Bass tracks by Marcus Gee
Drum tracks by Luke Bocchetta
Photography by Becca Brown
Printed by Book Printing UK

Introduction

The relatively short life span of the electric bass guitar has been an extremely progressive one. With pioneers in the 60s such as Monk Montgomery, Larry Graham and Louis Johnson introducing new concepts and ideas for the instrument for solo purposes, the evolution of the bass was launched into quicker motion. During the 70s, greats such as Stanley Clarke and Jaco Pastorius took bass playing to the next level turning the instrument into the centre focus of a band situation. Thus the bass was liberated from its status as a humble support instrument. The development of the instrument has continued with masters such as Victor Wooten, Marcus Miller and Michael Manring.

This book, as the title suggests, is aimed at the more experienced player wanting to practice and develop their advanced techniques or learn new techniques to enhance their playing. Its purpose is also to inspire creativity in the player's own composition, engendering new methods and a fresh approach.

Contents

Techniques

1.	Slap and Pop	1
2.	Finger Picking Chords	4
3.	Using Harmonics in Chords	8
4.	Two Handed Tapping	12
5.	Pinched Harmonics	18
6.	Artificial Harmonics	21
7.	Lap Style	24

Pieces

1.	Sable be Said	29
2.	Ship's Already Sailed	33
3.	La Geminiere	36
4.	You're Telling Me?	39
5.	Angora Bait	44

Harmonics: Fretboard layout, notation and tablature	49
Nomenclature (symbols)	51

Slap and Pop

Slap and pop is a technique generally used in funk, disco, soul and related genres. The slap involves a string (normally one of the lower two E or A) being struck by the bony part of the thumb. The pop part of this technique is created by snapping one of the strings (typically one of the higher two D or G) upwards with the index or middle finger.

The players that are generally credited for creating this technique on the electric bass are Larry Graham and Louis Johnson. Graham has said in several interviews that he was trying to emulate a percussive instrument before his band found a drummer. Players that are noted for using this technique include Stanley Clarke, Les Claypool (Primus), Michael Balzary (Flea – The Red Hot Chili Peppers) and Marcus Miller.

Slap and pop Ex. 1. After getting comfortable with finger style, slap and pop is normally the first advanced technique a student will learn. There are two ways to slap - overhand and underhand. The advantage of using overhand means it is easier to slap more than one string at the same time. The advantage of underhand means you can pluck the string with an up-stroke from the thumb immediately after striking the string. It is beneficial to use more than one finger to pop as it allows for smoother sounding lines. These exercises are designed for the practice of the technique and for inspiring different rhythms. We'll start off with a simple groove using both the index and second finger to pop.

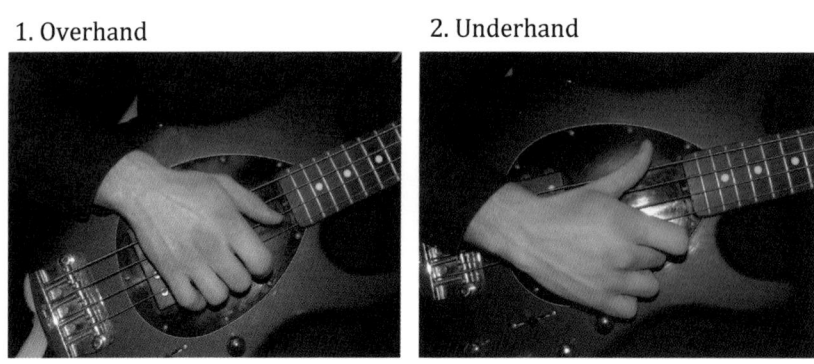

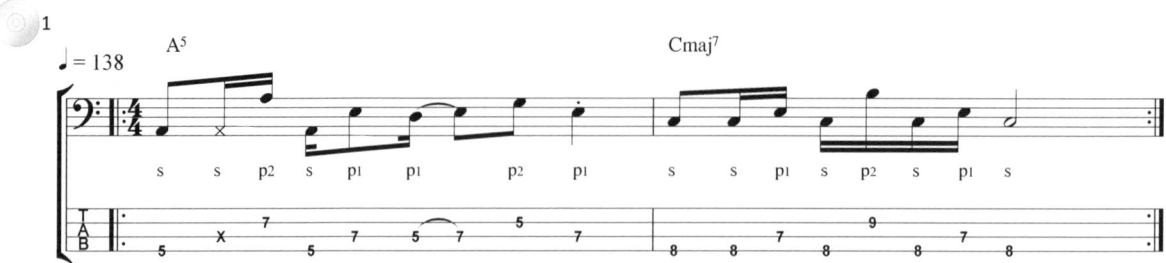

Ex. 2. Using hammer-ons for quicker rhythms.

Ex. 3. This rhythm is slightly more challenging. Hold a minor 7 shape and try to keep the thumb 'bouncing' all the time.

Ex. 4. Syncopation and more deadened notes.

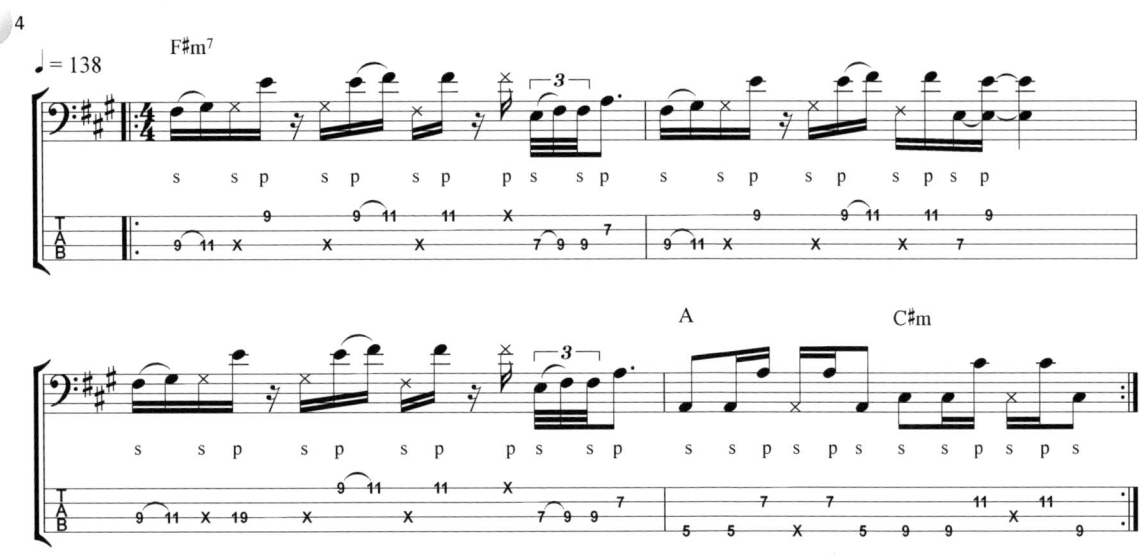

Ex. 5. This exercise concentrates more on the continual percussive sound with deadened 16ths for a tight groove.

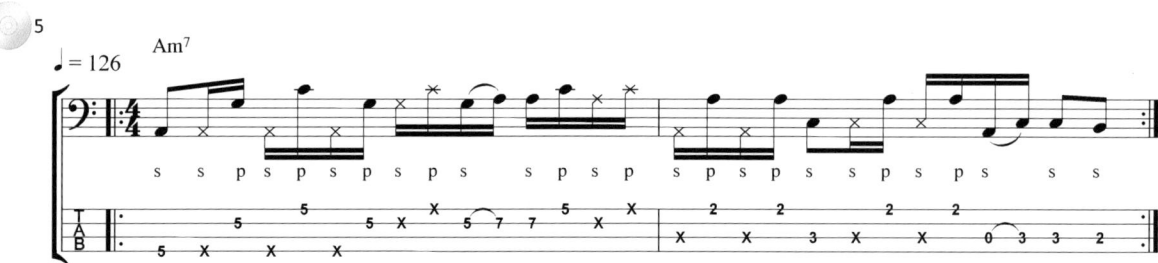

Ex. 6. Using a combination of hammer-ons and constant movement from the dominant hand, varying rhythms can be achieved.

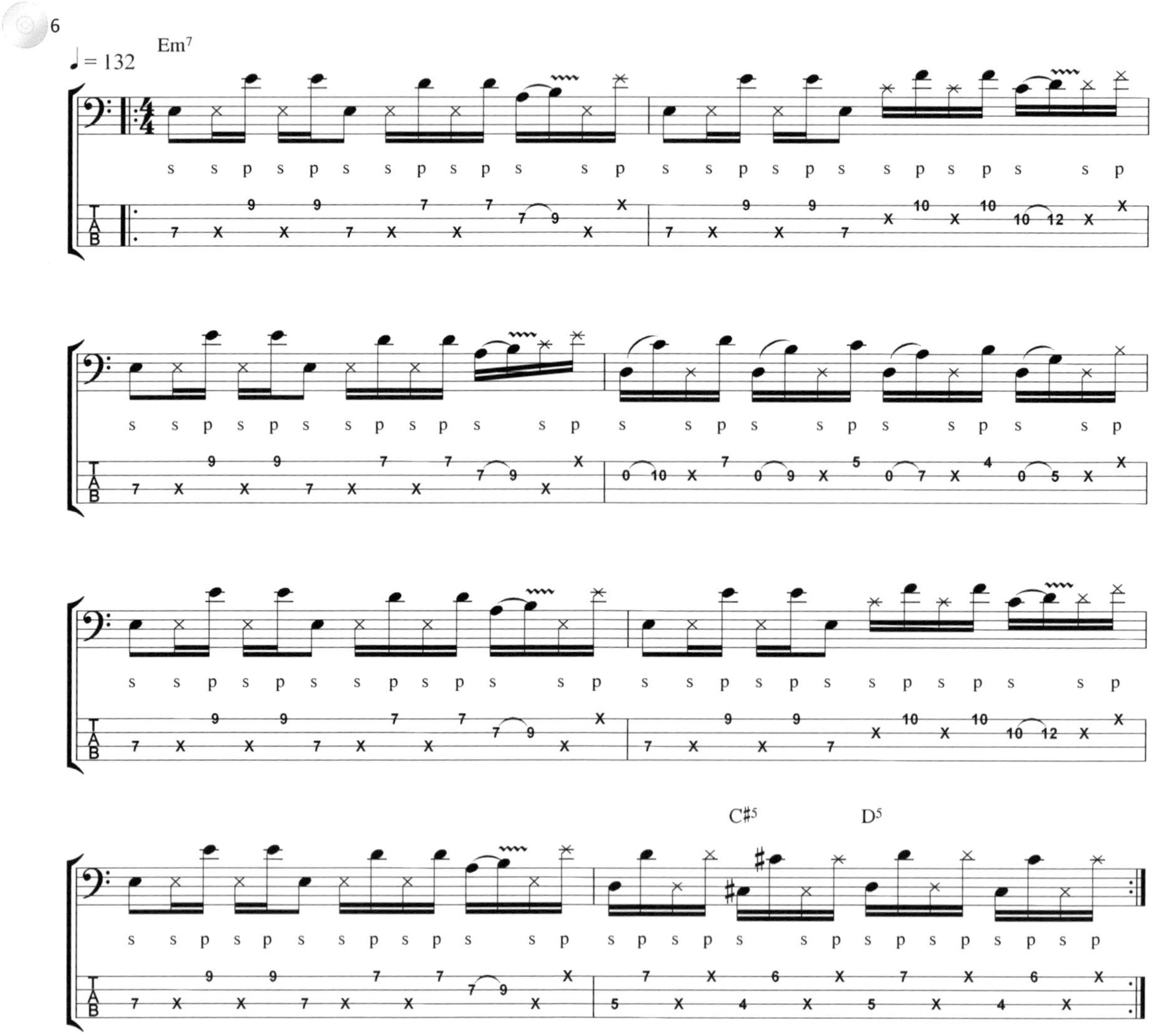

Finger Picking Chords

Finger picking chords is a standard popular guitar technique. It has been used since polyphonic stringed instruments first emerged. It became popular during the medieval period with instruments such as the lute and then some centuries later with the ukulele and the guitar. Playing chords on the bass is uncommon in a band situation but it is a polyphonic instrument and playing chords effectively will fill out rather than muddy the sound.

Amongst others, players such as Anthony Jackson and John Patitucci use this technique effectively for chordal passages in solo performances and with an ensemble.

Finger picking chords Ex. 1. The aim of these exercises is to practice holding different chord shapes and picking with the thumb and the fingers. Use the thumb for the bass notes and the index and second fingers for the higher intervals.

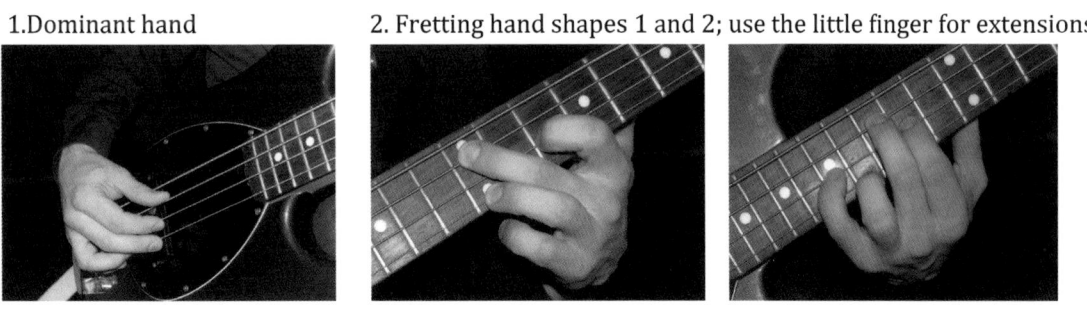

1. Dominant hand
2. Fretting hand shapes 1 and 2; use the little finger for extensions

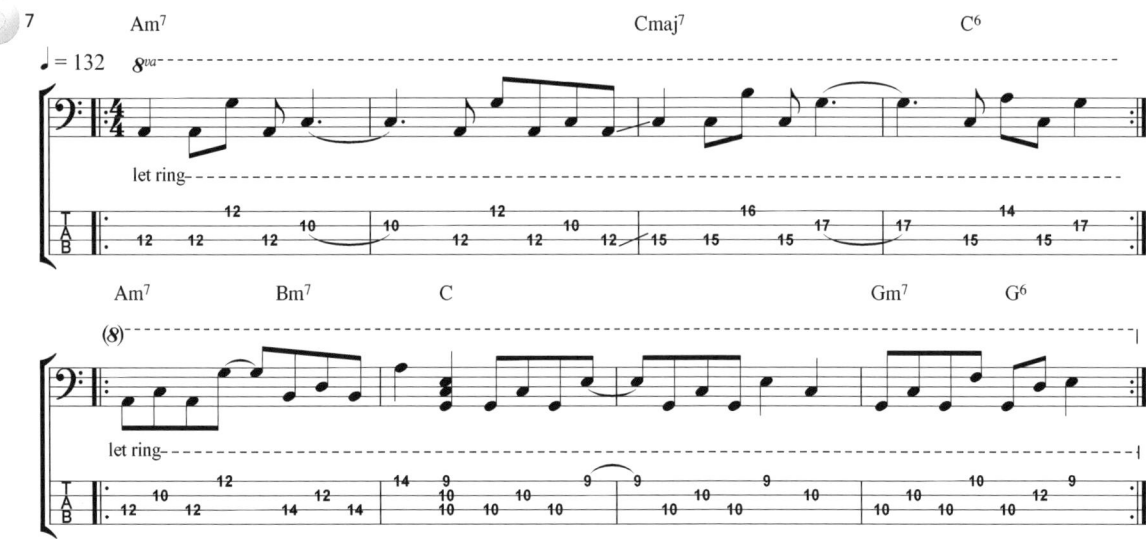

Ex. 2. Use up-strokes with the thumb to accurately achieve the correct timing at the beginning of bars 1 and 3.

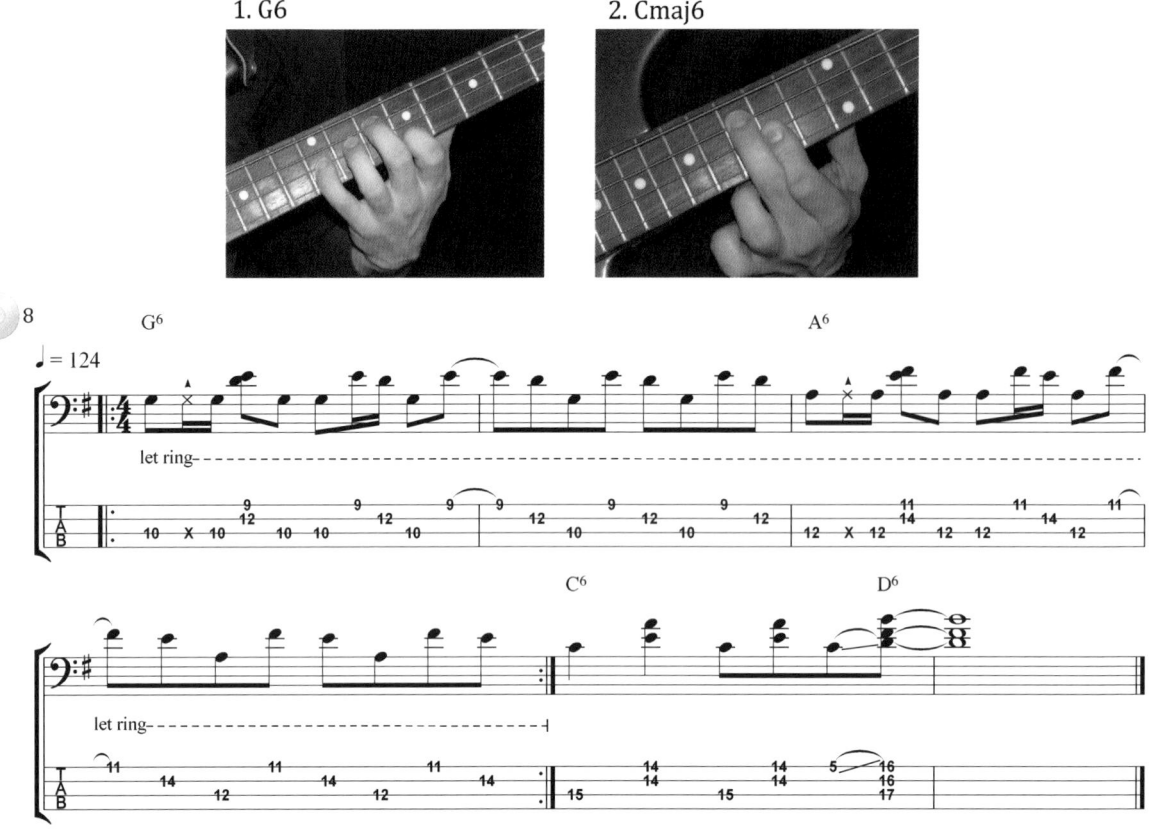

Ex. 3. Use the same shape for each chord but break position to play the fill at the end of the bar.

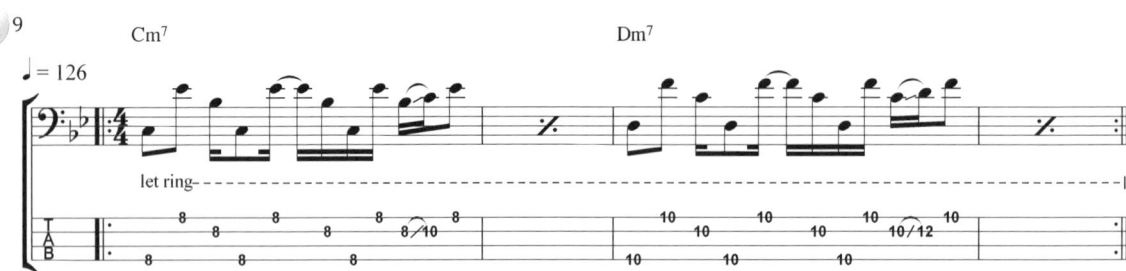

Ex. 4. So far we have used just the thumb and the 1st and 2nd fingers. Using three fingers means that finger picking patterns with four note chords are more accessible. Use one finger per string for this exercise, practice getting comfortable using the third finger.

1. Em11

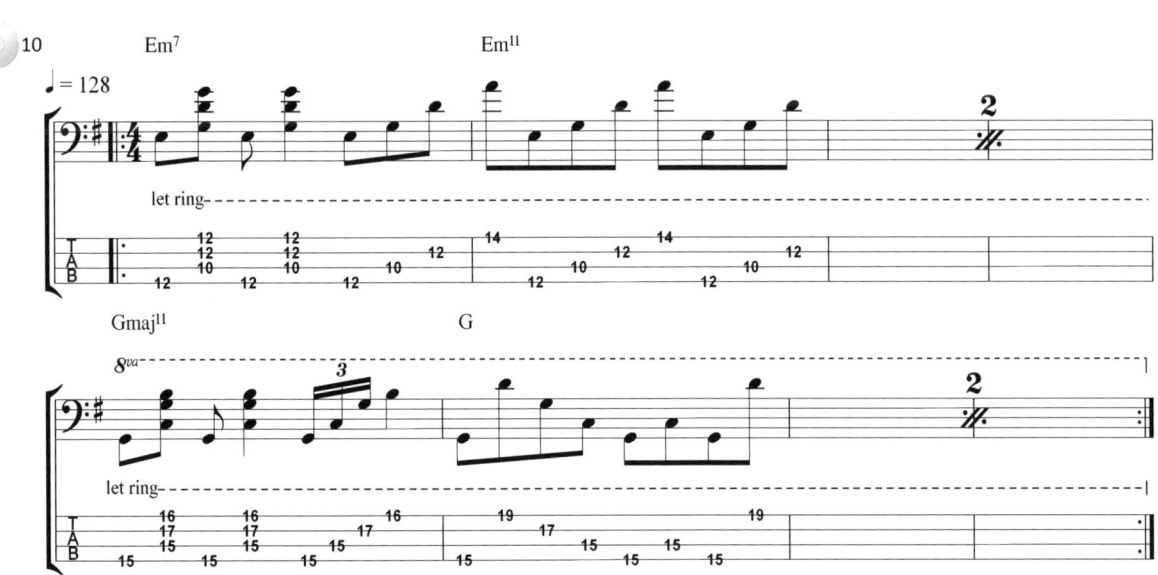

Ex. 5. Slap is largely considered an aggressive way of playing, however it can be used effectively to pick chords. Whilst still creating a percussive effect, the following exercise has more of a melodic approach rather than an aggressive one.

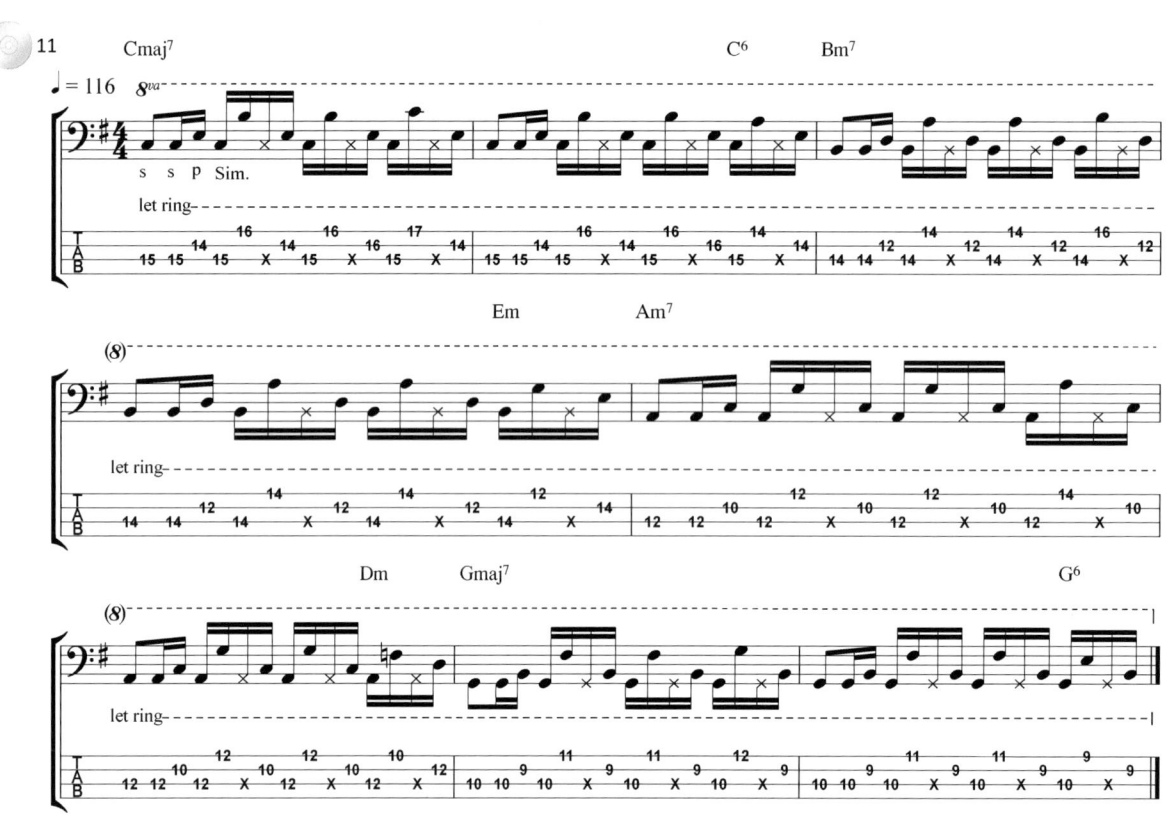

Ex. 6. A combination of slap and finger style for picking chords can also be very effective.

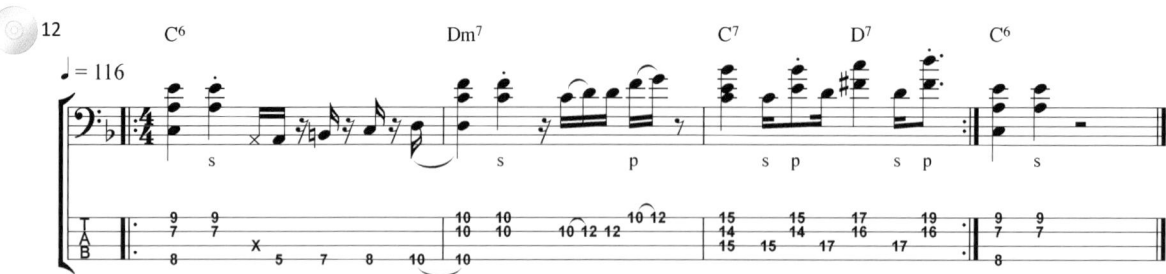

Using Harmonics in Chords

When chords are played on the bass they can sound muddy especially lower down the fretboard. A good way to avoid this is to replace the intervals with harmonics. However, the harmonics are often in a different place to the bass notes so there are certain limitations to easily achieving some chords. Using harmonics as an accompaniment means that notes can ring out allowing the player to continue with a bassline, adding harmony and texture to the piece.

'Portrait of Tracy' by Jaco Pastorius (1976) demonstrates the great potential of using natural harmonics on the electric bass; until this time most bassists had only used harmonics for tuning.

Using harmonics in chords Ex. 1. Starting simply, the first few exercises show how effective harmonics can be when used to create chords.

1. Fretting hand; keep fingers arched to let the harmonics ring out.

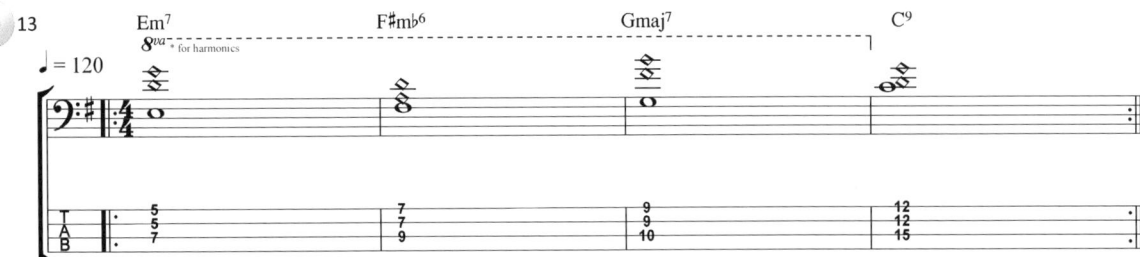

Ex. 2. Some more challenging shapes.

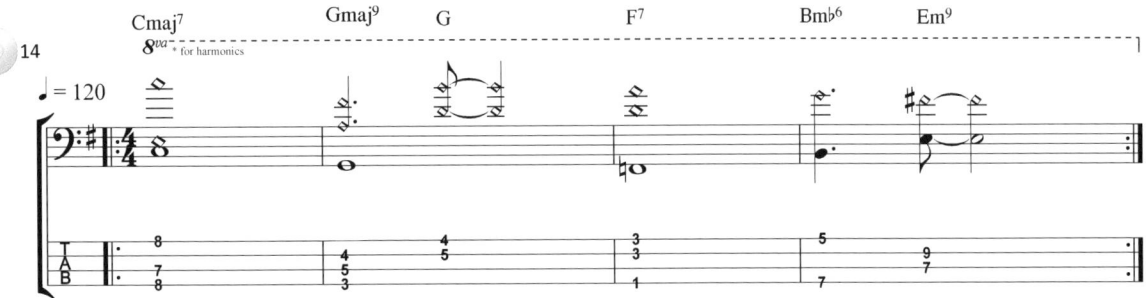

Ex. 3. Each chord in this exercise uses a different finger to play the bass note; a couple of these will be a little more awkward than the chords in previous progressions.

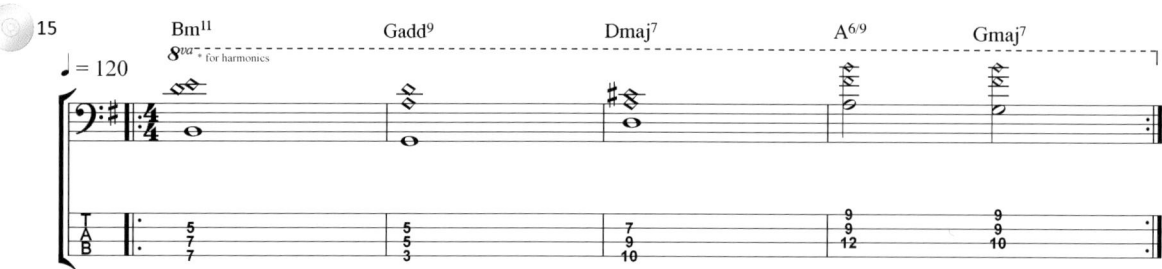

Ex. 4a. An advantage of using harmonics is that they will ring out when the fretting finger is lifted, enabling the space in between to be filled with bass lines and fills. Start by playing the chord sequence and then embellish the space to complete the bass line.

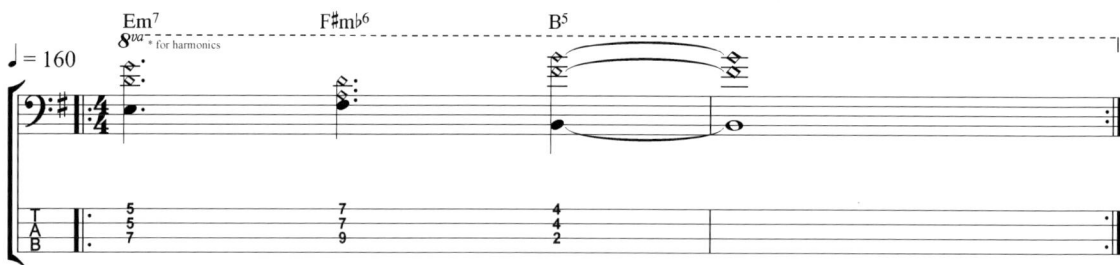

Ex. 4b. Embellishing the space.

Ex. 5a. This way of playing has great potential when playing solo or when you need to add textures to a piece. There are many possibilities for developing your basslines with this technique.

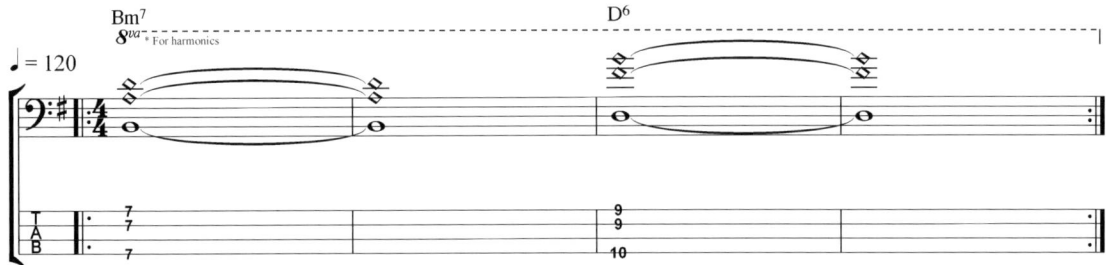

Ex. 5b. Adding a bassline.

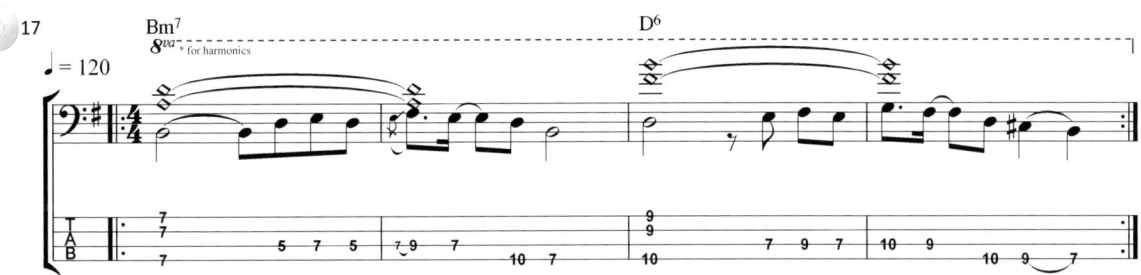

Ex. 6. The following exercise uses harmonics in a different way; instead of playing them simultaneously they are used within a finger picking passage to add harmonic texture.

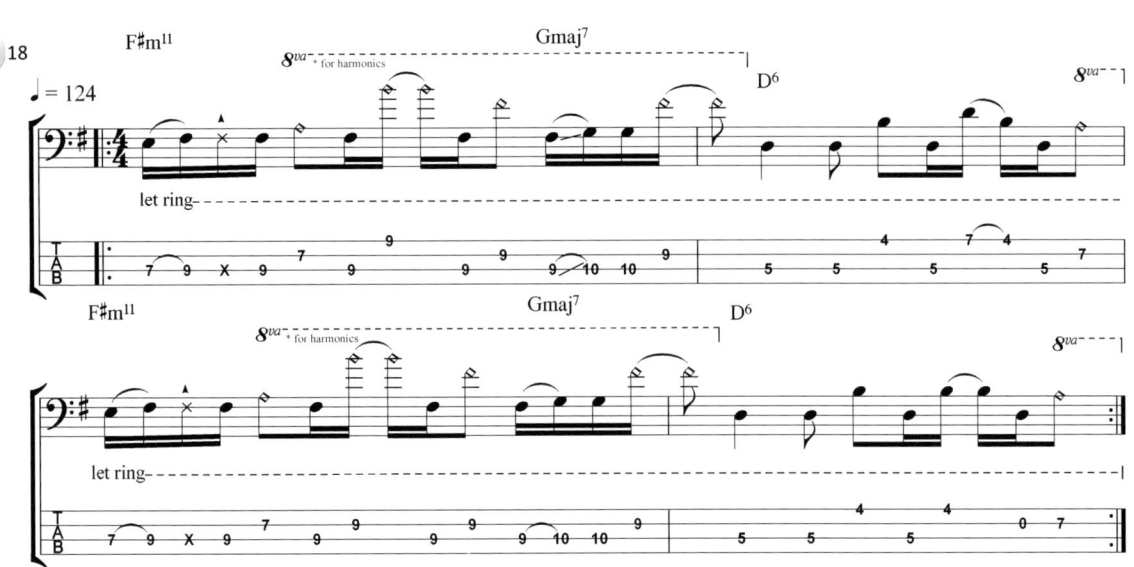

Ex. 7. A combination of these principles.

Two Handed Tapping

An early exponent of this technique was Harry DeArmond who used it to show off the sensitivity of his pickups in the 1930s. Later, in August 1969, Los Angeles based jazz guitarist Emmett Chapman discovered a new way to maximise the capabilities of the technique by tapping with both hands perpendicular to each other from opposite sides of the neck. This led to his invention of the Chapman Stick; a 9-string long-scale electric guitar.

Two handed tapping is an extremely useful technique for playing solo pieces. The technique was popularised on bass in the mid eighties by Billy Sheehan and Stuart Hamm and more recently by Victor Wooten and Michael Manring, all of whom continue to use the technique to great effect. The technique allows the player to perform two separate lines or to accompany their bassline with double stops or chordal progressions. When using this technique imagine how you would play a piano and press the notes down firmly to attenuate any buzzing.

Two handed tapping Ex. 1. Start by exercising both hands cycling up and down a major scale to get used to this method of playing, be firm when hammering on to minimise fret noise. After getting a bit more comfortable it is good practice to play through different scales to get all the fingers working in different positions. Try playing through all the modal scales in the same way.

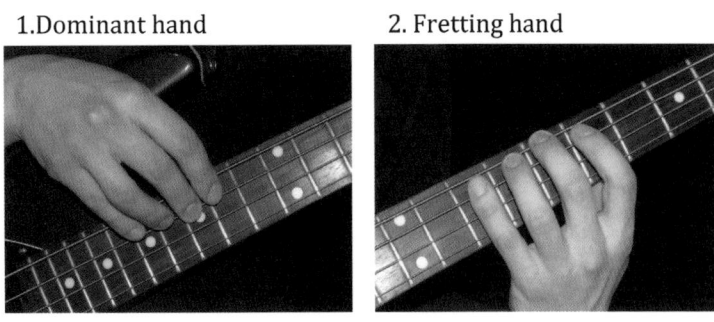

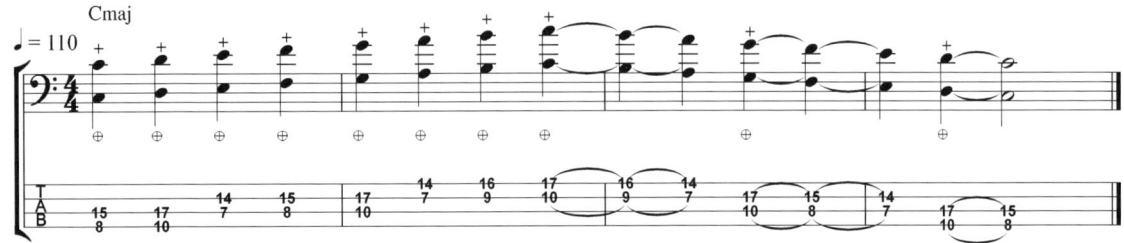

Ex. 2. Now try to play chords using both hands. Using this technique makes it possible to achieve many different chords without sounding muddy as the notes can be spaced out across the fretboard.

1. Dominant hand major 3rd
2. Fretting hand perfect 5th

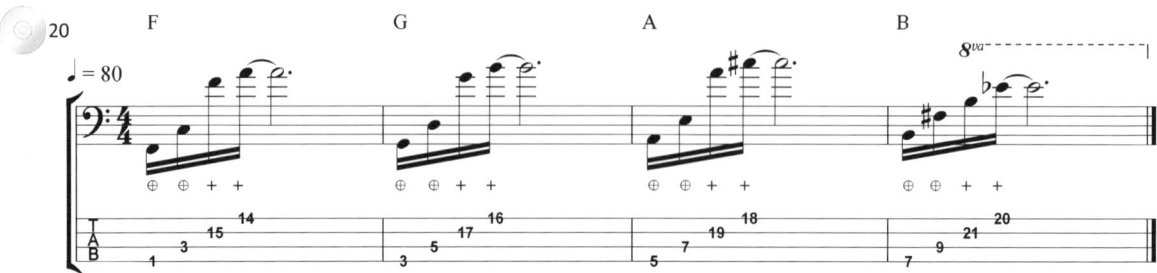

Ex. 3. Major 7 chords.

1. Dominant hand major 3rd and major 7th

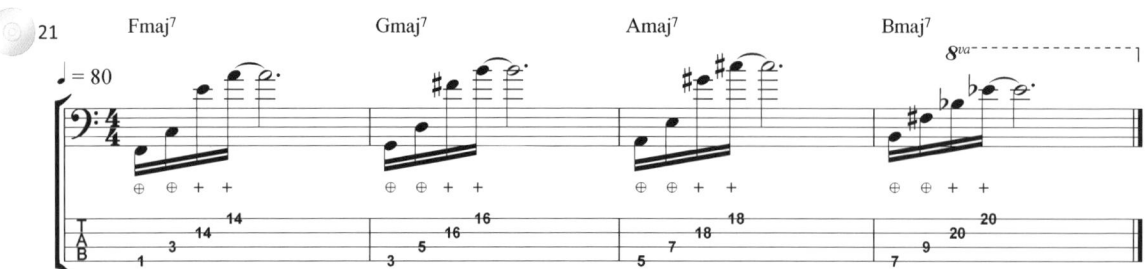

Ex. 4. This exercise involves playing a combination of chords and a simultaneous line.

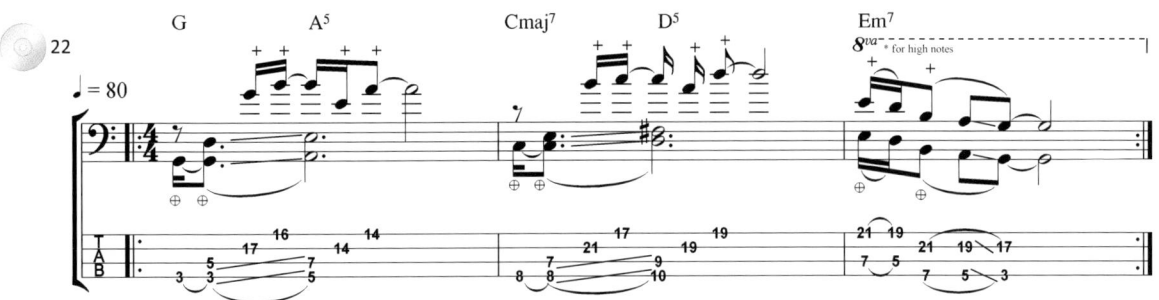

Ex. 5a. When you are comfortable tapping with both hands try these exercises. They involve two different rhythms played at the same time using double stops to create a chord progression. Try each part separately starting with the fretting hand.

Ex. 5b. Dominant hand double stops.

1. Dominant hand minor 3rd

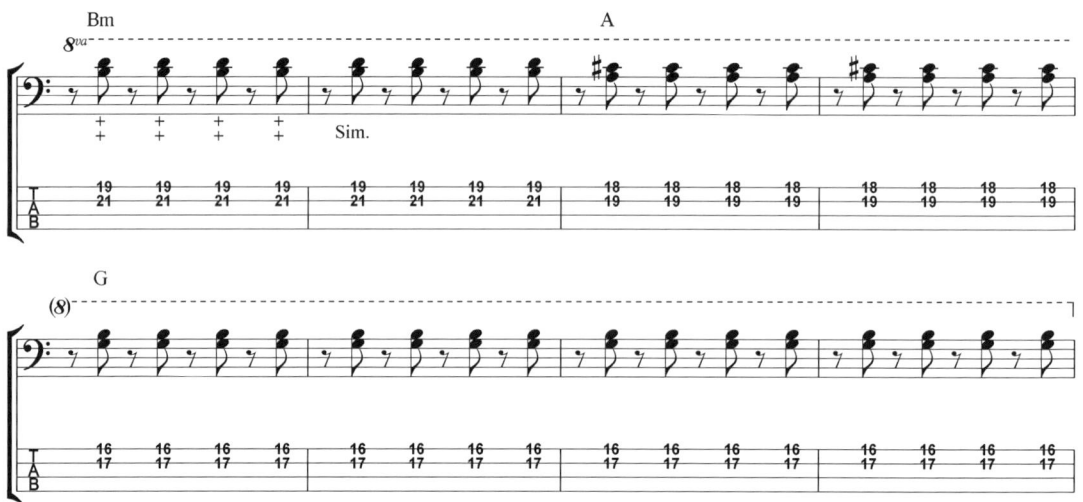

Ex. 5c. The parts together.

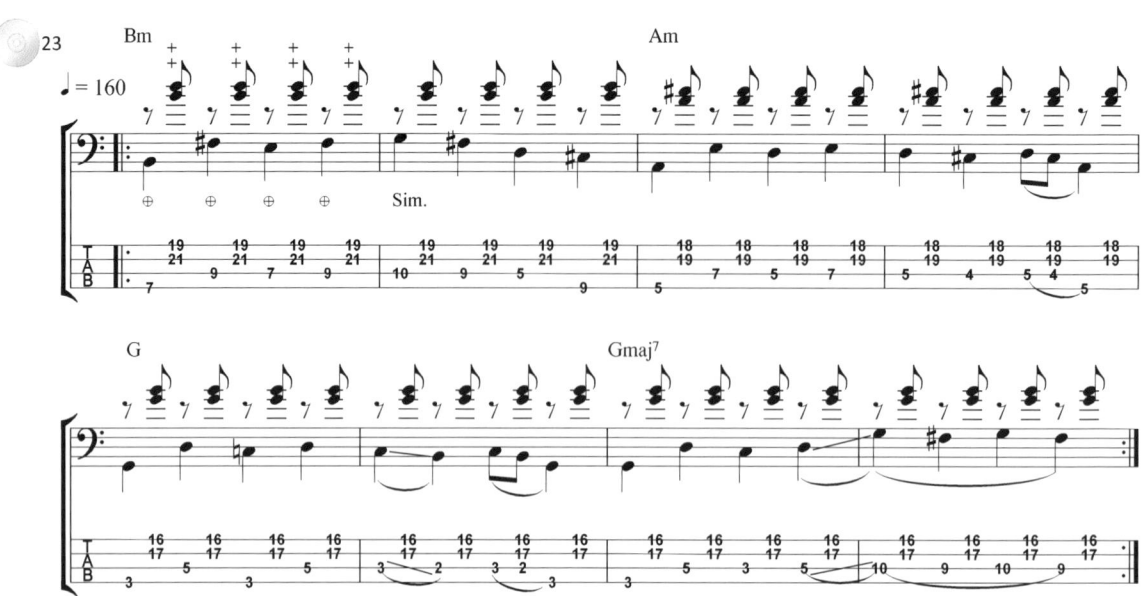

Ex. 6a. This exercise comprises more of a Latin rhythm from the bass line and the double stops.

Ex. 6b. Dominant hand double stops.

Ex. 6c. The parts together.

16

Ex. 7a. The following exercise comprises a more strenuous bass line and uses sustained double stops to fit the groove.

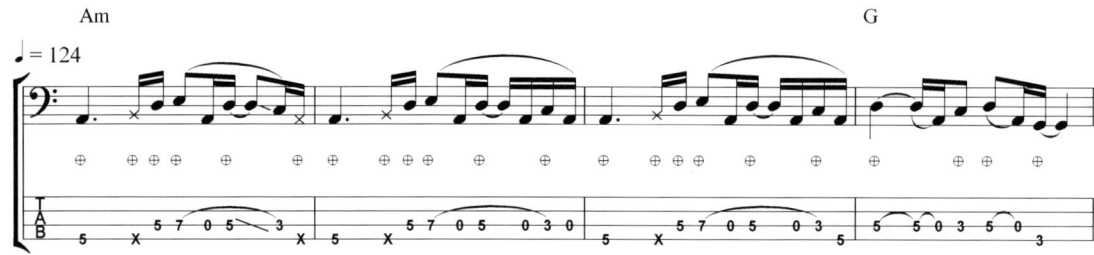

Ex. 7b. Dominant hand.

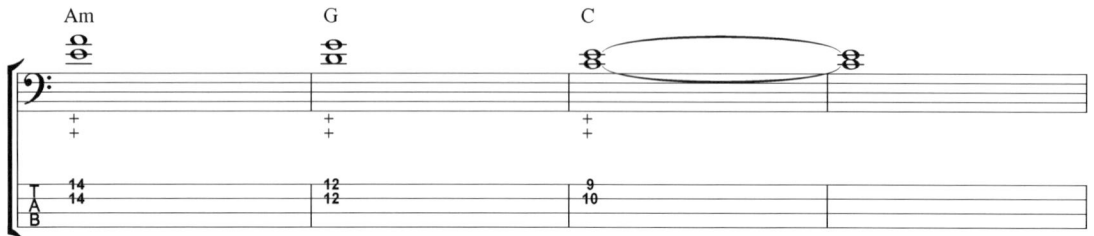

Ex. 7c. The parts together.

Pinched Harmonics

Pinched harmonics are possible on any fretted stringed instrument; these are also known as squelch picking, picked harmonics or squealies. They are achieved by plucking the string and holding either the index finger or thumb over a harmonic position. If the index finger is used to 'pinch' the harmonic, the ring finger usually plucks the string; if the thumb is used, the index finger usually plucks the string.

This technique is most widely used by electric guitarists playing rock and metal music where plenty of distortion ensures that the more subtle harmonics are greatly amplified. An early example of this technique can be heard in Roy Buchanan's 1962 recording of 'Potato Peeler'. Robbie Robertson learned the technique from Buchanan and has used this style of playing on many of his classic guitar solos with The Band. Another prime example of this technique is Jerry Garcia of the Grateful Dead in 'Loser' from their May 8, 1977 show. The technique has been adopted by bass guitarists and is utilised very effectively by the likes of Michael Manring, Victor Wooten and particularly Jaco Pastorius on his solo piece 'Portrait of Tracy'.

Pinched harmonics Ex. 1. Harmonics are also found higher than the end of the fretboard. Using a pinched technique, these harmonics can be played more easily. Practice using these prominent harmonics to increase your accuracy. It may take some trial and error to find the exact location of the higher harmonics; use the tab as a guide. Use either the first and ring finger or the thumb and first finger of the dominant hand.

1. Using the fingers.

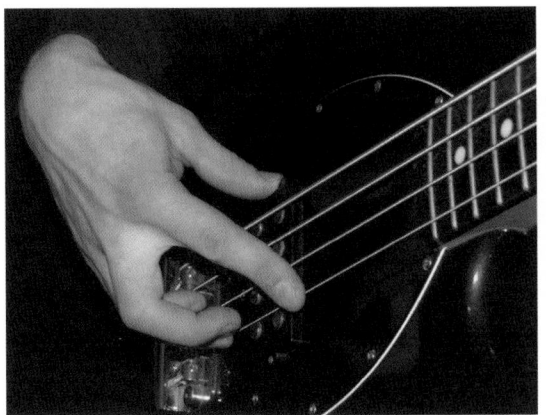

2. Using the thumb.

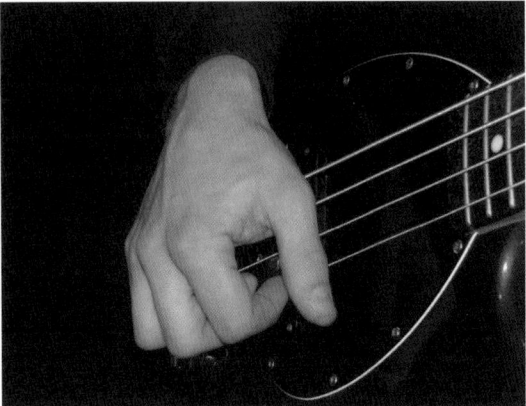

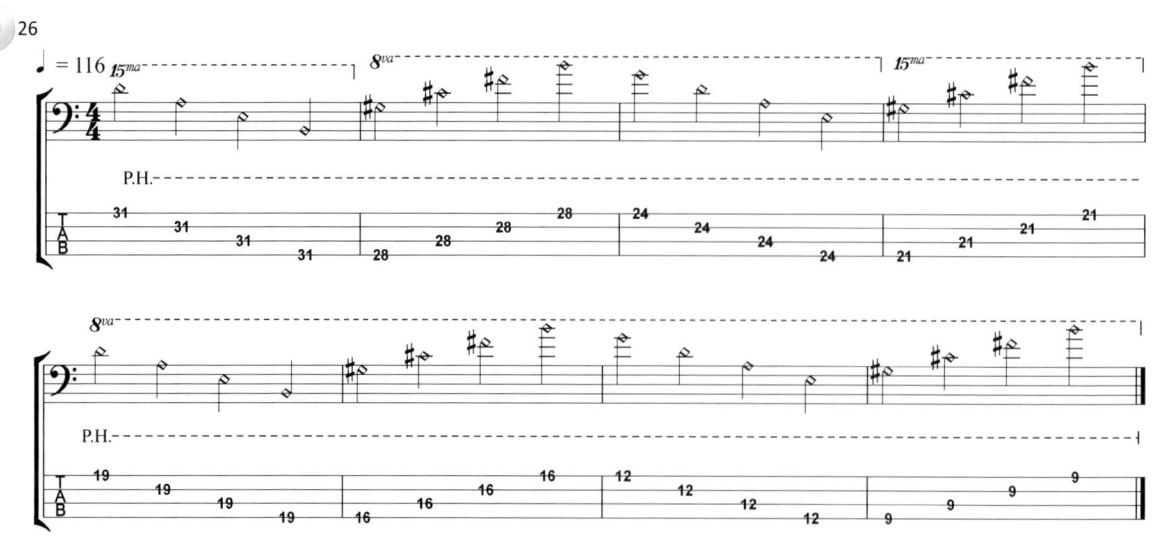

Ex. 2. Using two fingers to pluck the harmonic can be a very effective way of playing pinched harmonics rapidly. If you're using the first finger to hold over the node, alternating between the third and second finger to pluck will probably feel unnatural at first but it's a technique worth developing.

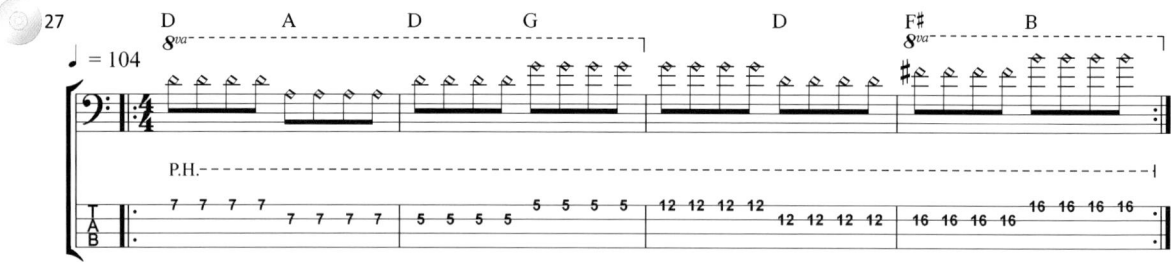

Ex. 3. We know that using harmonics and bass notes together produce a rich sound. Using pinched harmonics allows you to play harmonics anywhere on the fretboard whilst playing bass notes at another position. Play the bass notes with the thumb whilst using the alternating finger technique for the pinched harmonic quavers.

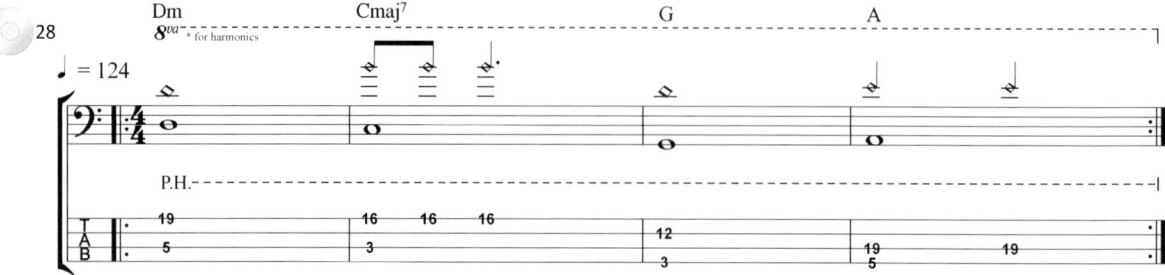

Ex. 4a. It is possible to develop this method much further by bringing in a range of harmonics and playing different bass lines. We'll look at the next exercise in two stages.

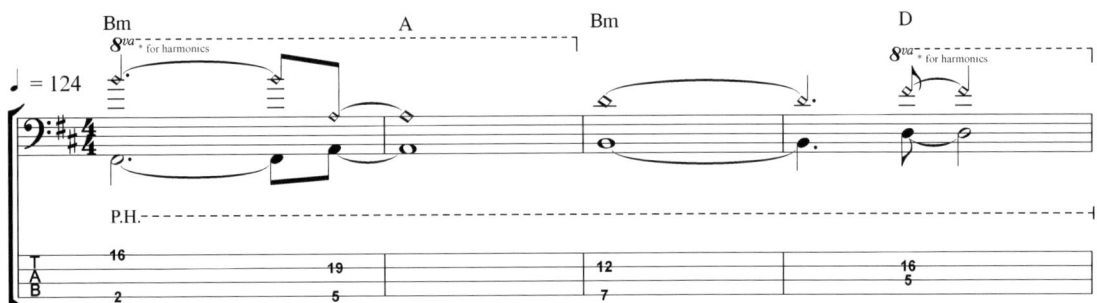

Ex. 4b. Adding a groove.

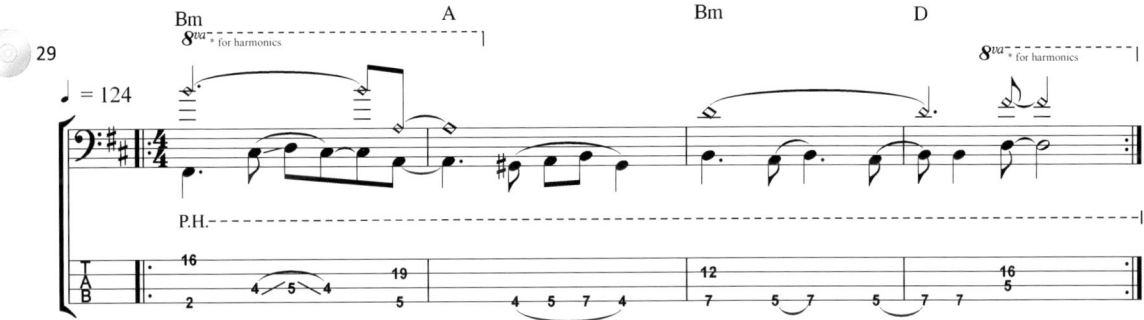

Ex. 5. This technique allows you to become very inventive with your bass lines and it is a very valuable method when playing solo.

Artificial Harmonics

Artificial harmonics are a good way to play in a higher register. It is possible to achieve any note in the form of a harmonic using this technique, whereas some harmonics are difficult or even impossible to accomplish naturally or pinched. To play an artificial harmonic, fret a note normally and pinch or tap a harmonic on the same string. The easiest harmonic will be the octave position but other harmonics can also be achieved. When fretting a note and playing artificial harmonics, all of the harmonic positions will change but the intervals between nodes will remain the same.

This method enables a wide range of harmonics to be played as the fretted position can be changed. It also allows the player to add vibrato to the harmonic by bending the fretted string. Artificial harmonics are notated with two note heads; the bass note shows where the fretting hand is and the diamond note head shows the actual pitch of the harmonic.

Artificial harmonics feature in Jaco's 'Portrait of Tracy'. Many bassists, including Micheal Manring and Steve Bailey, make good use of this technique for different timbres in their performances on fretless and fretted basses.

Artificial harmonics Ex. 1. The easiest harmonics to play are an octave above the fretted position. Let's use a major scale to practice moving both hands at the same time and becoming accurate with the dominant hand.

Ex. 2. The Ionian mode using artificial harmonics. Practice this method using all the modal scales to help increase accuracy on all strings.

Ex. 3. A simple bassline's timbre can be changed using artificial harmonics. Try playing the following simple groove with and without artificial harmonics and listen to how different the lines sound.

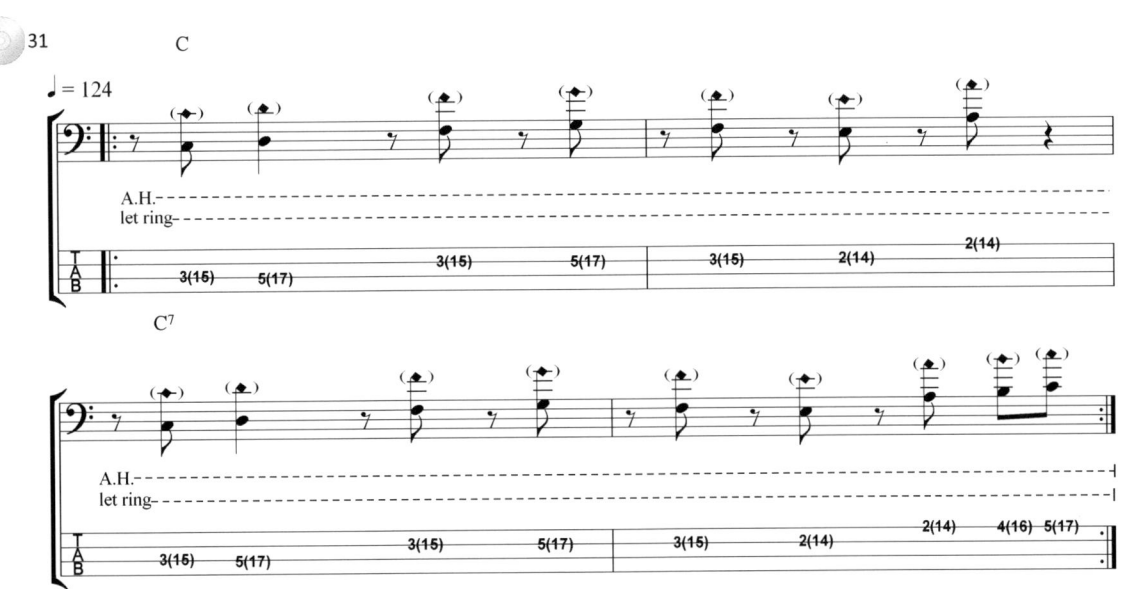

Ex. 4. Some lines can immediately sound more melodic when they are transposed to a higher register. Many harmonics can be achieved other than just the octave when the fretting hand remains in the same position. The following exercise introduces this concept.

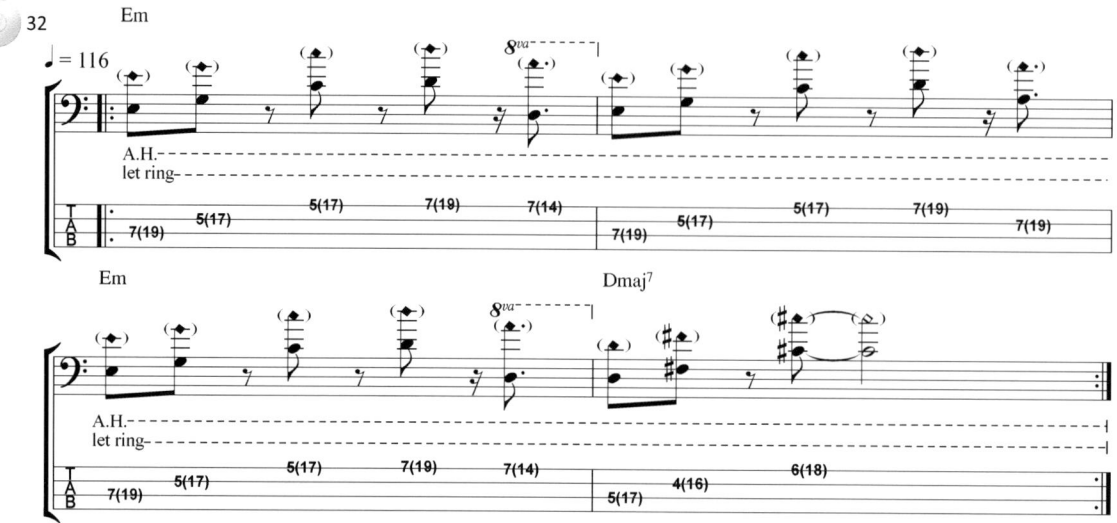

Ex. 5. This exercise develops the idea further with different harmonics for the same fretted position and includes some harmonics located higher than the range of the fretboard. This is a fiddly piece which may require a bit of practice to achieve accuracy.

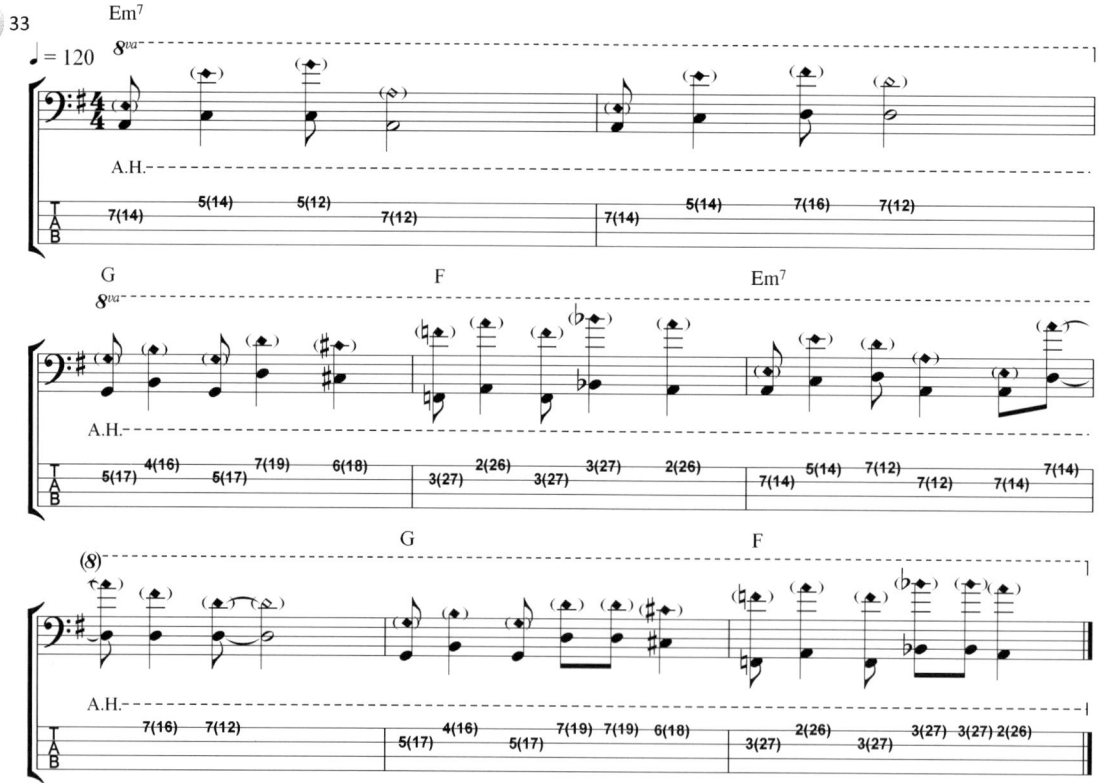

The harmonics you play with this technique can also be tapped which makes accuracy more difficult but adds a percussive element by striking the node with the tip of the first or second finger. It is good practice to try these exercises again using the tapped technique as this comprises a valuable method for lap style; to be introduced in the next section.

Lap Style

Lap and percussive styles of playing the bass are rare, the technique has evolved from slide guitar typically used in the blues. A man named Joseph Kekuku is thought to have invented the lap steel guitar in 1885. It is said that at the age of 7 Kekuku picked up a metal bolt and slid it along the strings and was intrigued by the sound. He taught himself to play using this method with the back of a knife blade. Subsequently guitars were adapted to be played horizontally. The instrument become popular in the States in the 1920s and 1930s. Guitarists then started to play normal acoustic guitars on their laps for the ease of adding percussive sounds simultaneously with melody. John Paul Jones is noted for performing with a custom made lap steel bass.

This style is a very modern and innovative way of playing the acoustic bass. The next few exercises are short grooves to inspire you with this method of playing. The usefulness of this technique in a small ensemble and the possibilities it provides to perform solo can be very valuable.

Lap style Ex. 1. This is a technique not taught in the grading system. By positioning the bass across the lap and playing overhand with the fretting hand, beats, melody and a bassline can be played at the same time. I have put together a few exercises to introduce the idea and the basics of the technique. Start by tapping the artificial harmonics and then bring in the beat with the elbow. Finally add the bass notes; the first two notes are played by hammering on with the thumb.

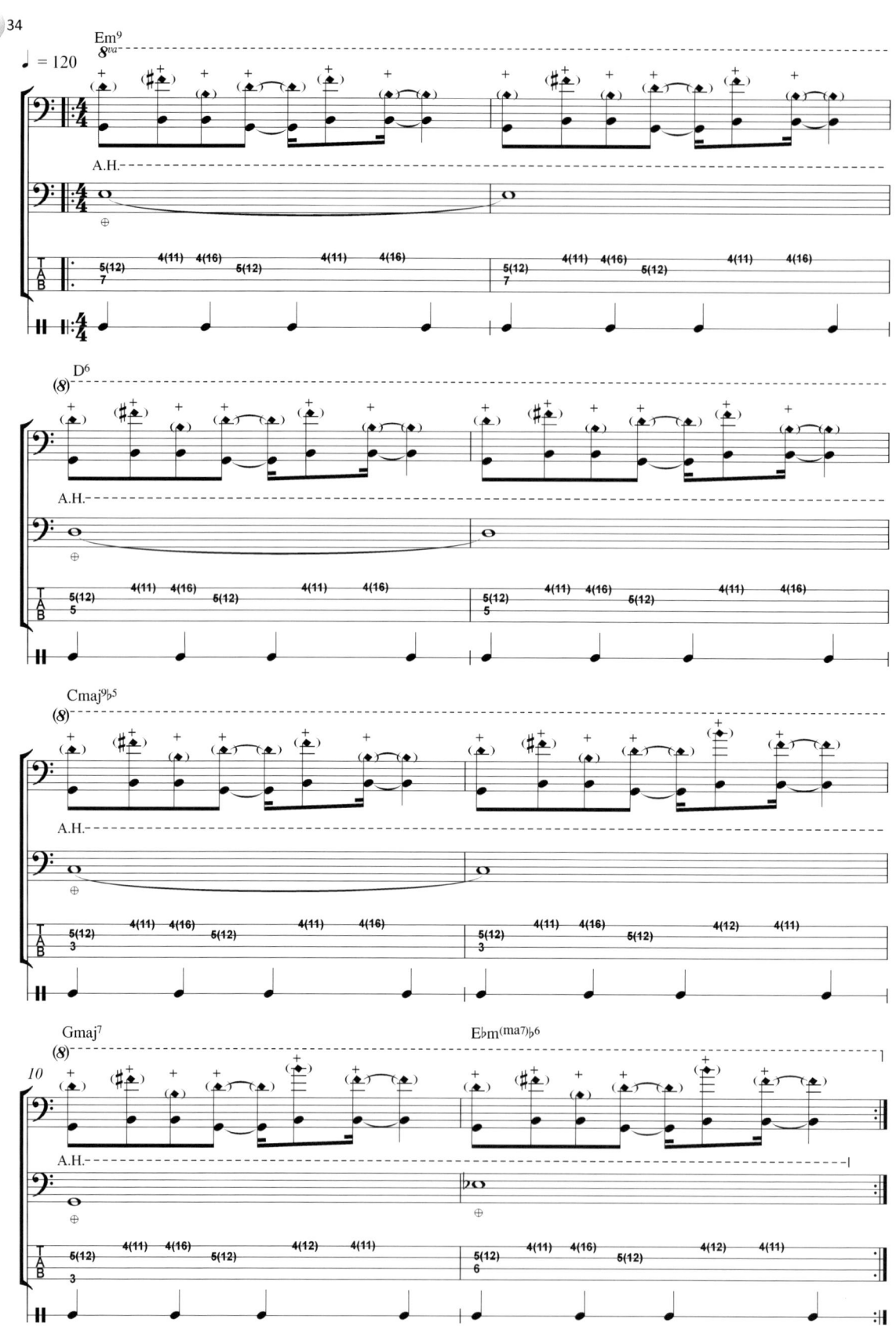

Ex. 2. This exercise shows how you can hold bass notes and tap harmonics using only the fretting hand. It allows you to play a more complex rhythm with the dominant hand using the elbow, the thumb and the fingers on the side of the body of the bass. Practice tapping the harmonics and holding the bass notes before adding the rhythm. Perform a twist of the wrist using the fretting finger as the pivot to achieve the power necessary to sound the harmonic.

Ex. 3. You can also tap harmonics in between beats or together with the beat of the elbow with the dominant hand, allowing the fretting hand to play a more complex bass line. This is a line that was introduced in an earlier chapter of the book; 'Using Harmonics in Chords'. It has been developed further with this technique.

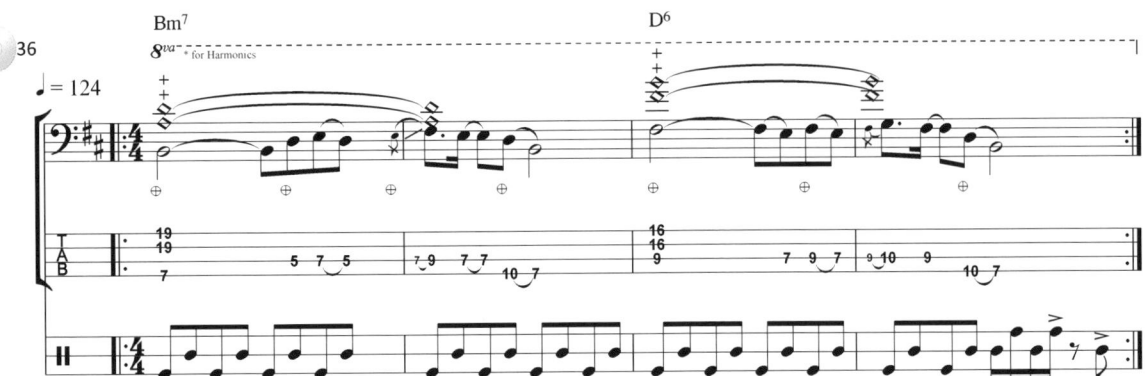

Advance Bass Tuition: Study Pieces

Composed by Marcus Gee

The following study pieces have been composed as solo bass pieces with drum accompaniment; together they contain the techniques that have been covered in this book.

Sable be Said

Marcus Gee. B.1990

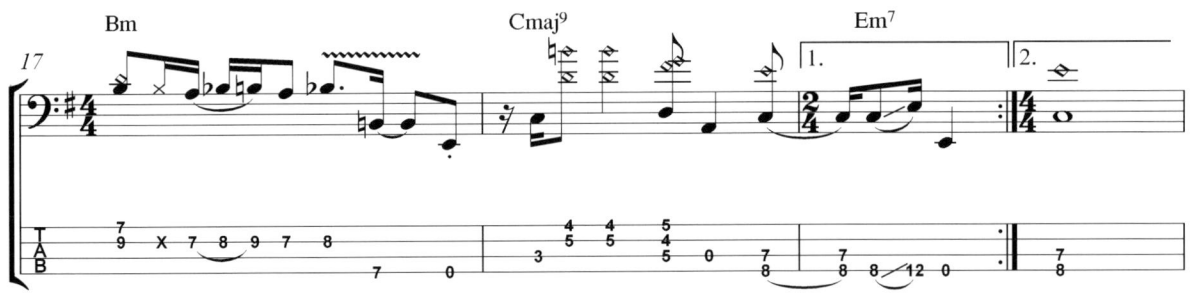
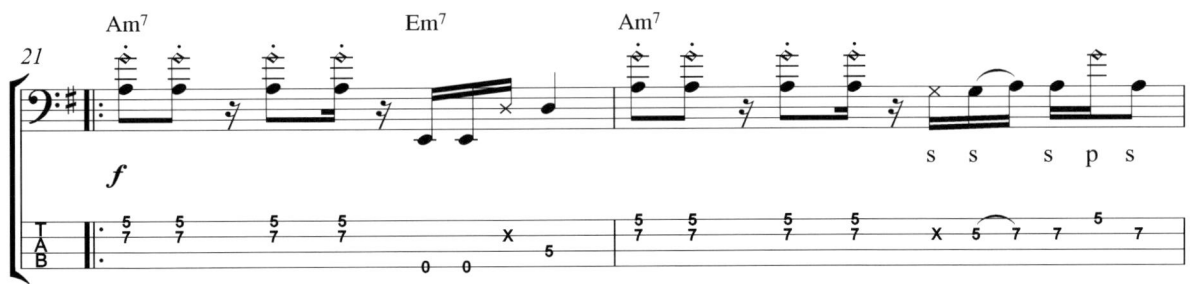
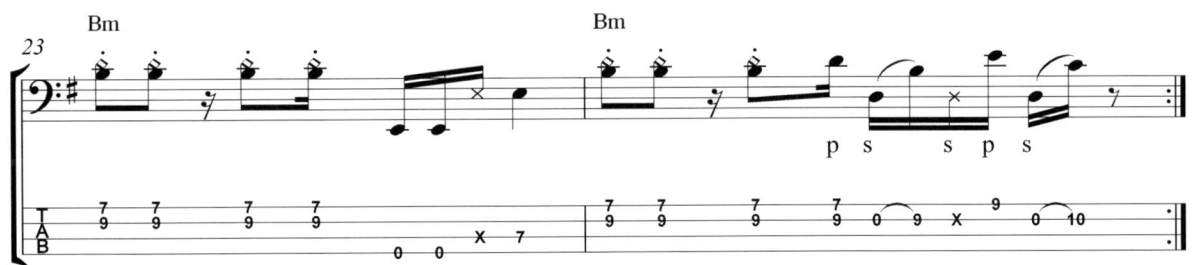
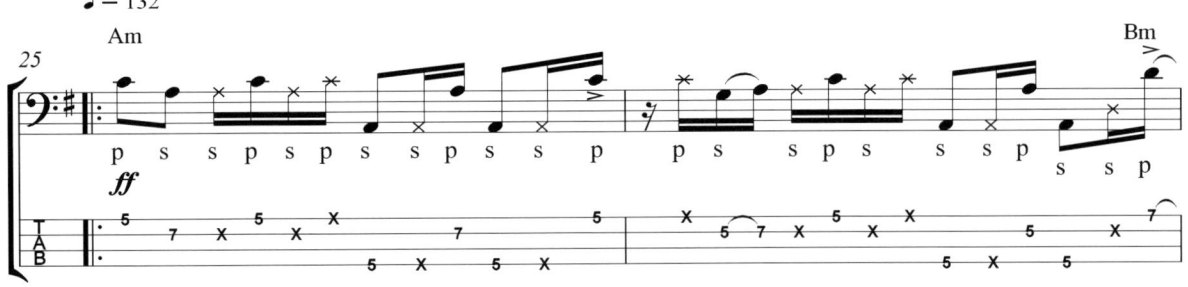
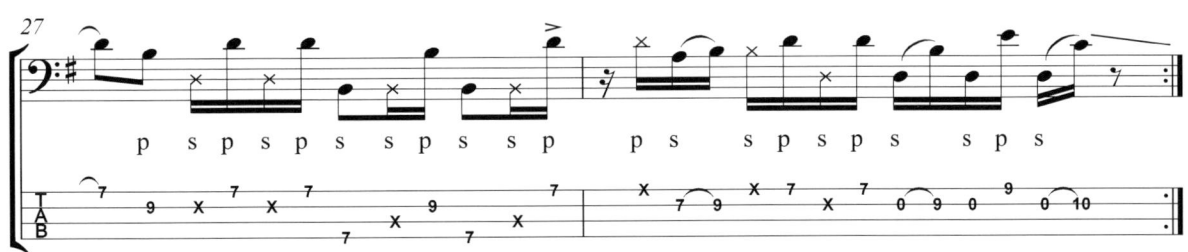

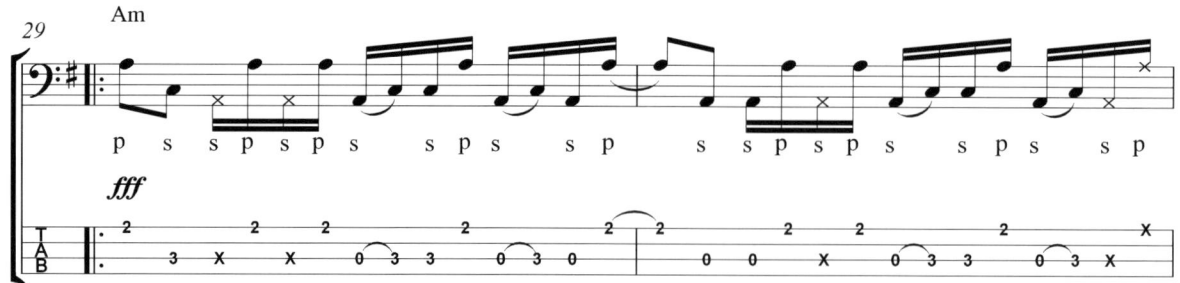
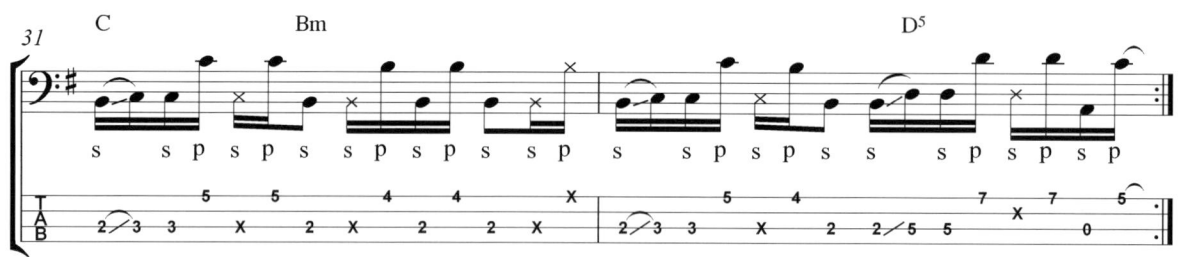
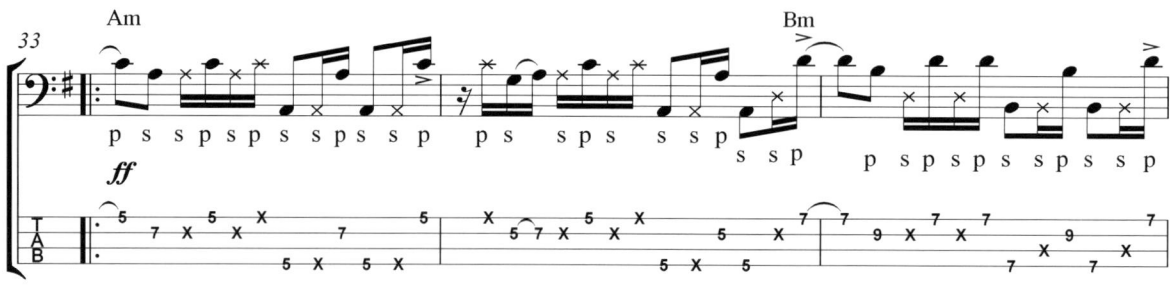
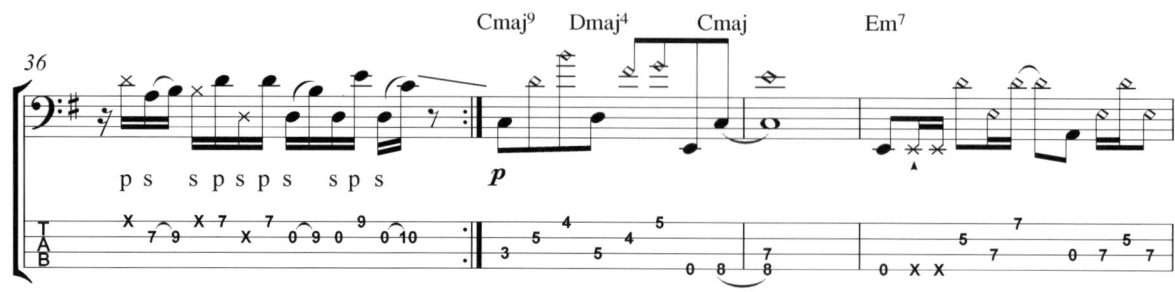
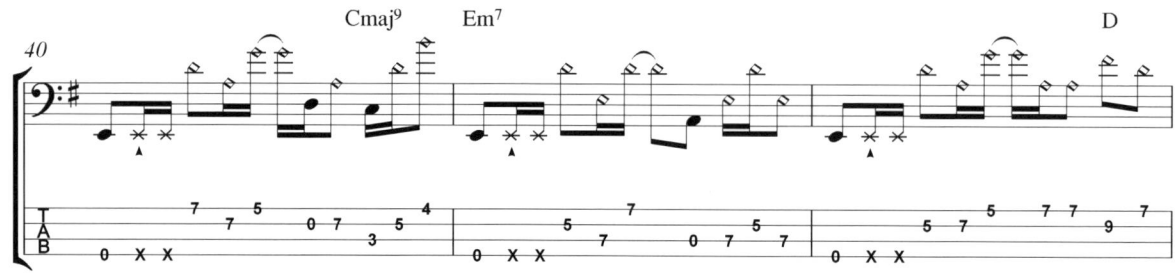

31

Ship's Already Sailed

Allegro ♩ = 124

Marcus Gee. B.1990

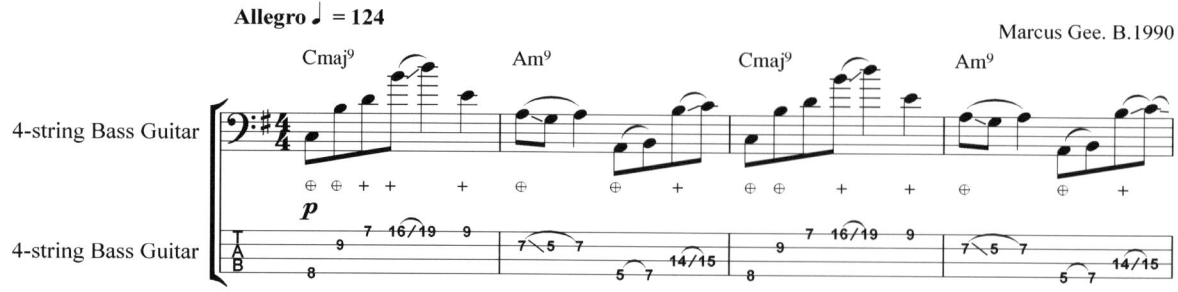
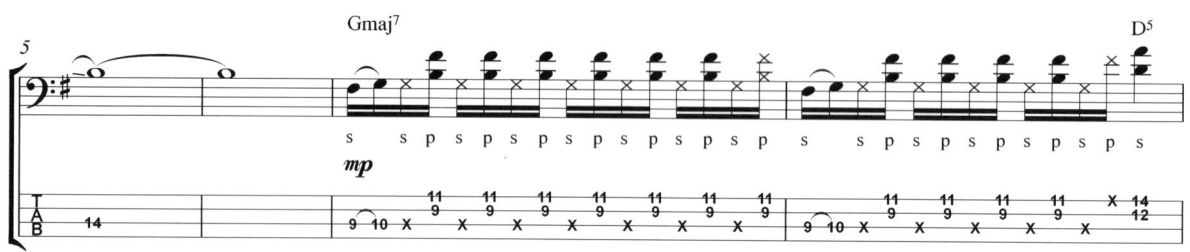
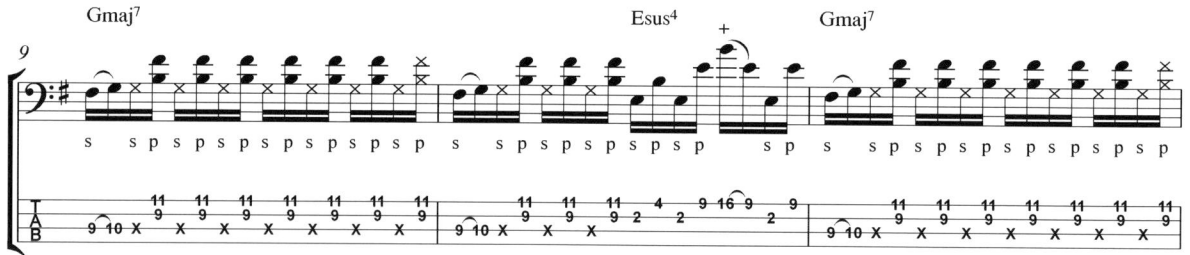
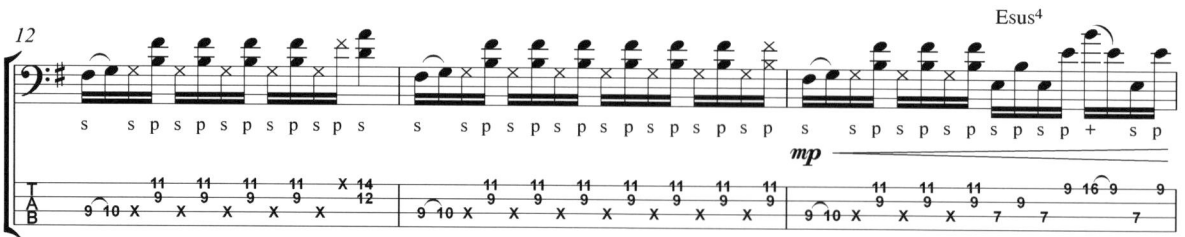
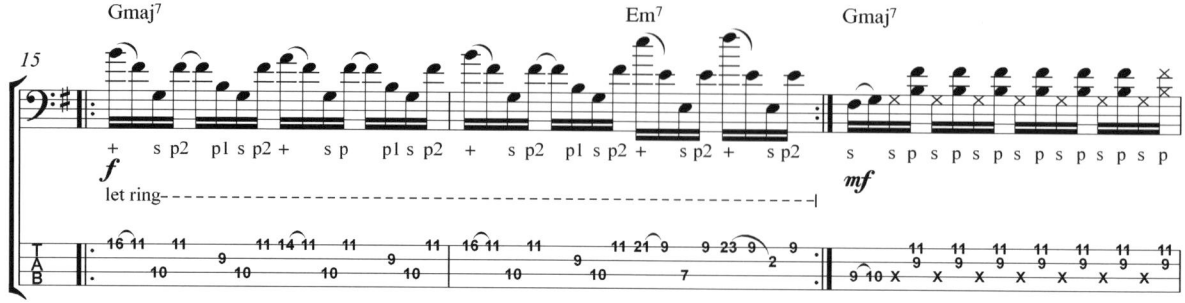

© Marcus Gee 2014

D5
Gmaj7
Em7
Gmaj7
D5
Gmaj7
Esus4
Gmaj7
Em7
let ring
Em
D
Let notes ring until the end.
Em
Em6
Dm
Dm6
Em
Em6
Dm
Dm6

37
Gm13
* Use a volume boost here (recording uses bass overdrive)
* Notes tapped with 1st and 3rd fingers of each hand
♩ = 226
ff
42
Sim.
Cm13
48
Gm13
52
Cm13
56
G5

La Geminiere

Marcus Gee. B.1990

15
Em7 Bm C Em7 G
17
Bm7 C♯m9
mf
3
19
Bm Cmaj7
21
F♯m♭6 Gmaj7 Em7
mf
24
Bm Cmaj7

27
Em7 Am Bm Em7 Am
f
29
Em7 Bm C Em7 G
31
Bm7 C♯m9 Em7 Cmaj7 Am
mf
mp
3
34
Em7 Cmaj7 Am F Fmaj7
15ma * for harmonics
2
Sim.
38
G Gmaj9 Em7
rall.
T
A
B

You're Telling Me?

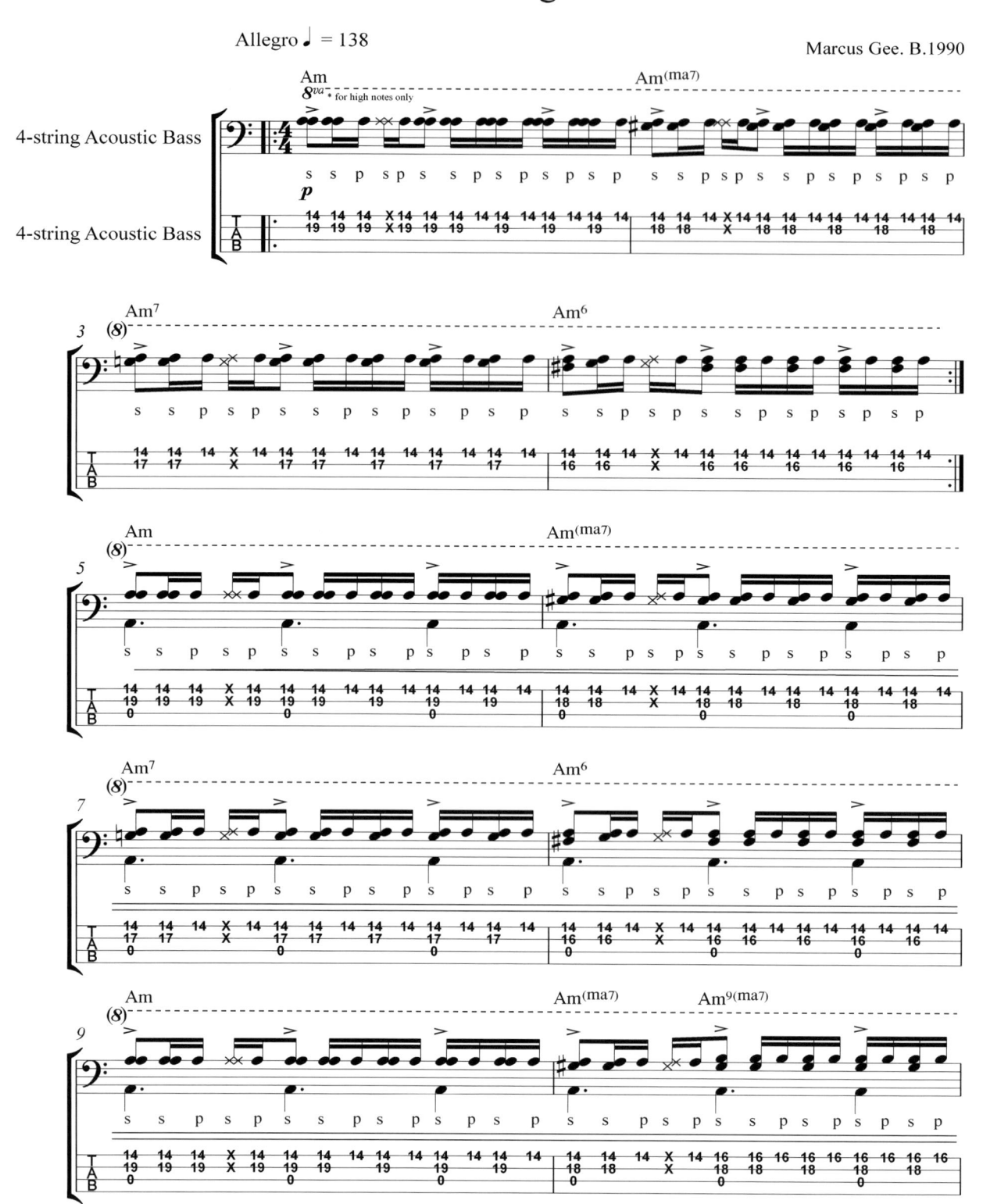

Allegro ♩ = 138

Marcus Gee. B.1990

Am7
Am6
A6
f
Am7♭6
mp
Sim.
Dsus4
Am♭6
ff
let ring
Dsus4
Am♭6
let ring
Am7♭6
mp
Sim.

Dsus4
Am♭6
Sim.
Let ring until strummed
Lap style
Am7
= 142
* for harmonics
A.H.

Am7
A.H.
Fmaj9
A.H.
A.H.
Am7
A.H.
Steady knocks on the body with the elbow
Perc.
Fmaj9
A.H.
Perc.

43

Angora Bait

Marcus Gee. B.1990

21
Em7
F♯m♭6
Gmaj7
mf
25
Emadd9
Gmaj7
Am7
Gmaj4
15ma
A.H.
29
Emadd9
Gmaj7
Am7
Bm
p
33
Em7
Em6add9
Em7
Em6add9
8va
ff
37
Em
Em11
A
1.
A
2.
8va
* Double stops
P.H.

42
Em7
F♯m♭6
Gmaj7
m
46
Em7
F♯m♭6
Gmaj7
m
50
Em7
F♯m♭6
Gmaj7
mf
54
Emadd9
Gmaj7
Am7
Gmaj4
A.H.
A.H.
A.H.
A.H.
58
Emadd9
15ma
Gmaj7
Am7
Bm
A.H.
A.H.
p

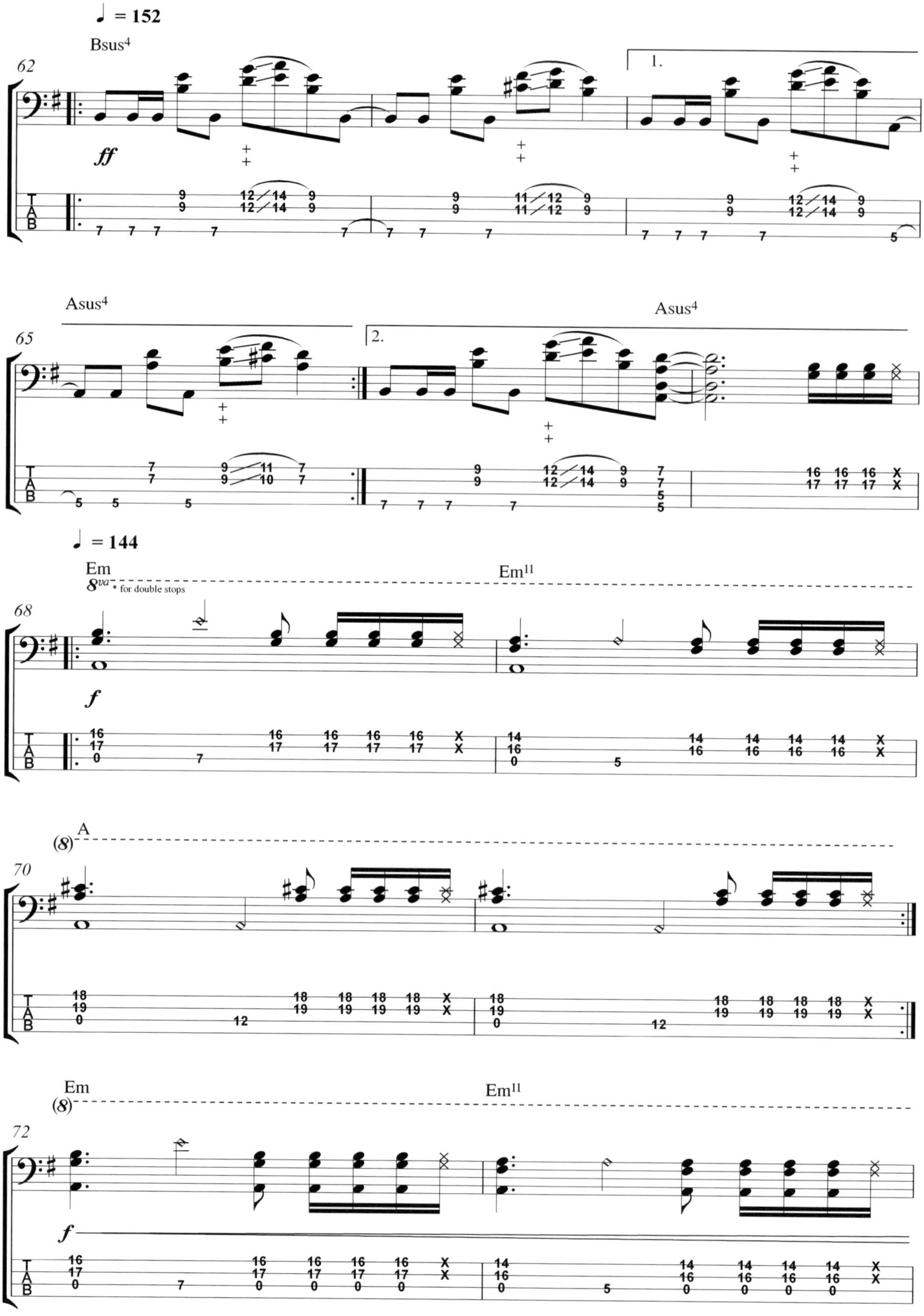
♩ = 152
Bsus4
62
ff
1.
Asus4
65
2.
Asus4
♩ = 144
Em
8va
* for double stops
Em11
68
f
A
(8)
70
Em
(8)
Em11
72
f

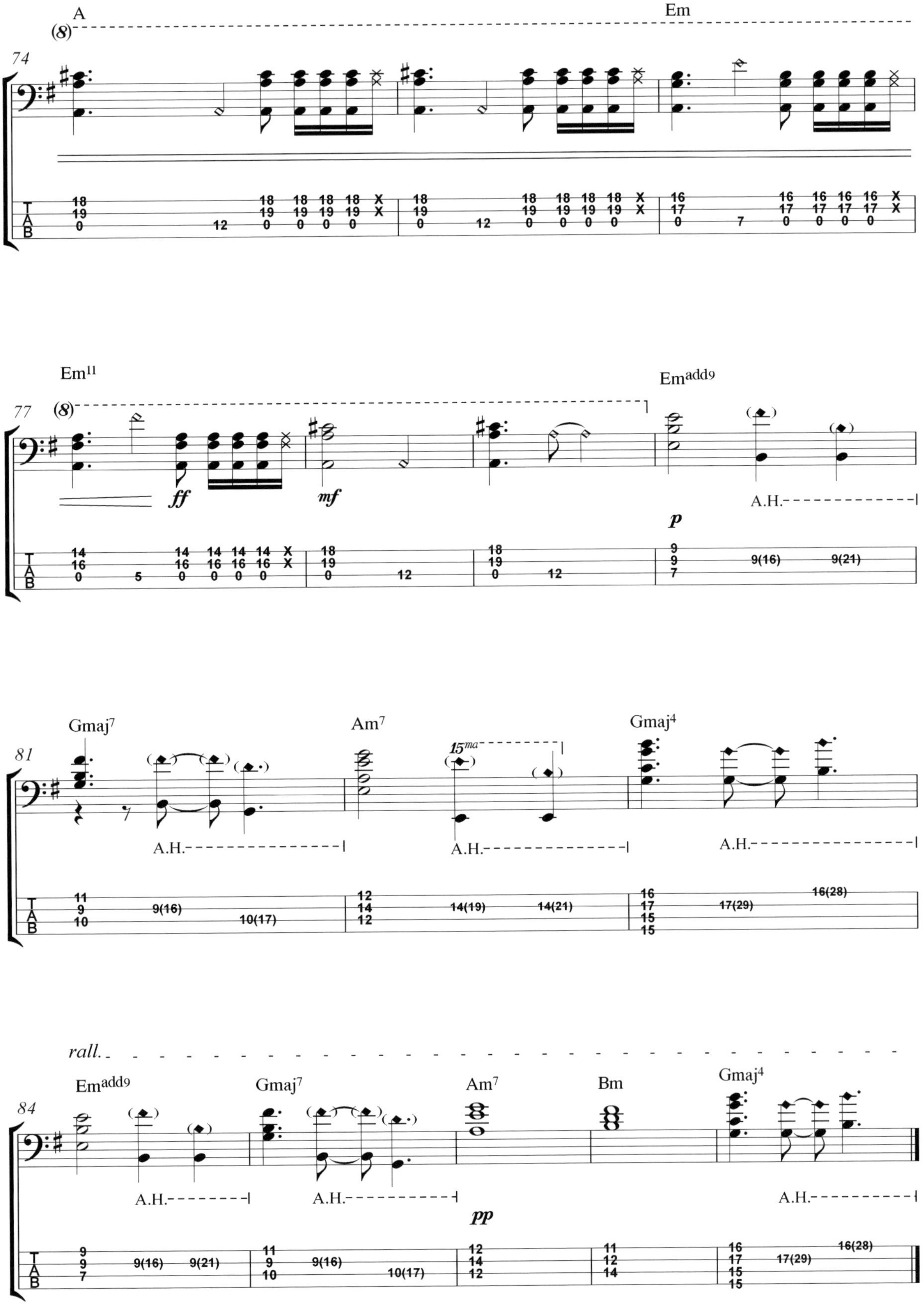
A
Em
Em11
ff
mf
Emadd9
A.H.
p
Gmaj7
Am7
15ma
Gmaj4
rall.
Bm
pp

Harmonics: fretboard layout, notation and tablature

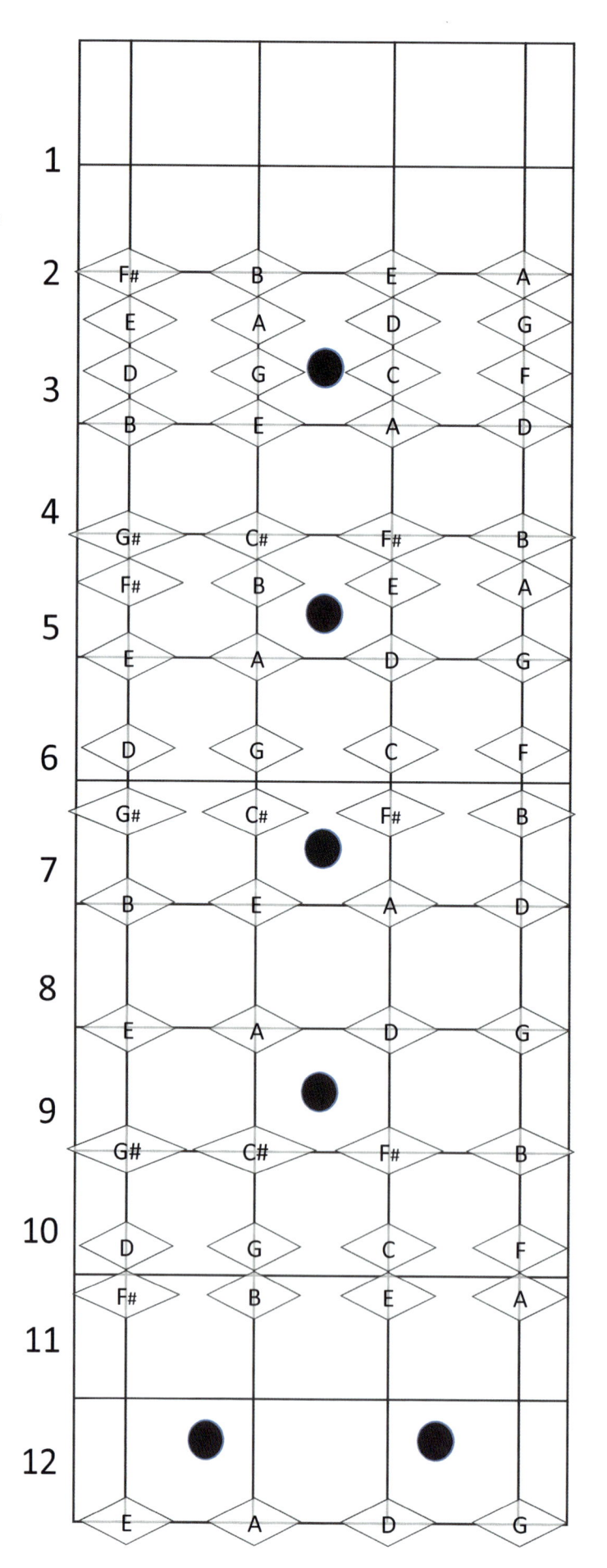

Fret				
2	F#	B	E	A
	E	A	D	G
3	D	G	C	F
	B	E	A	D
4	G#	C#	F#	B
	F#	B	E	A
5				
	E	A	D	G
6	D	G	C	F
	G#	C#	F#	B
7				
	B	E	A	D
8				
	E	A	D	G
9				
	G#	C#	F#	B
10	D	G	C	F
	F#	B	E	A
11				
12				
	E	A	D	G

49

15ma
F♯ B E A E A D G
2 2 2 2 3.2 3.2 3.2 3.2
(15)
D G C F B E A D
3.6 3.6 3.6 3.6 3 3 3 3
8va
G♯ C♯ F♯ B
4 4 4 4
15ma
F♯ B E A
5.2 5.2 5.2 5.2
8va
E A D G
5 5 5 5
15ma
D G C F
6.8 6.8 6.8 6.8
15ma
G♯ C♯ F♯ B
7.2 7.2 7.2 7.2
8va
B E A D
7 7 7 7
15ma
E A D G
8 8 8 8
8va
G♯ C♯ F♯ B
9 9 9 9
15ma
D G C F F♯ B E A
10.8 10.8 10.8 10.8 11.2 11.2 11.2 11.2
E A D G
12 12 12 12

Nomenclature

S = Slap - strike the note with the bony part of the thumb
P = Pop - hook finger under the string and pluck

p1 = Pop with the 1st finger
p2 = Pop with the 2nd finger

⋀ = Up-stroke with the thumb

◊ = Natural harmonics

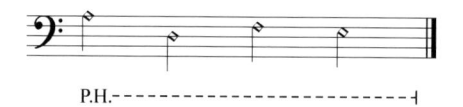

P.H. = Pinched harmonics

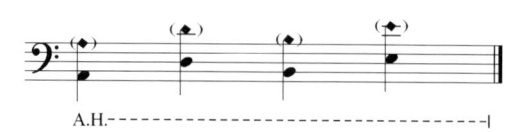

A.H. = Artificial harmonics
The lower notes indicate fretting position
The notes in brackets show the pitch of the harmonic

⊕ = Tap with fretting hand
+ = Tap with dominant hand

Perc.

Percussion stave.

Bottom line = Beat with the elbow
Middle line = Slap with the bony part of the thumb
Top line = Slap on the side of the body with fingers

Hammer-on   Pull-off   Slide

〜 = Vibrato - modulate the pitch of a note
by repeatedly bending and releasing the string
· = Staccato - note is played to sound short
> = Accent - note is played louder
× = Cross head - note is muted/deadened

8va for harmonics = Only the harmonics sound an octave higher

15ma for harmonics = Only the harmonics sound two octaves higher

8va for high notes = Only the high notes/line 2 sound an octave higher

8va for double stops = Only the double stops sound an octave higher

Marcus Gee has been a performing musician for 10 years, he gained a music scholarship at the University of the West of England and has recently graduated. He has professional experience as a musician across the board playing with many different bands and has extensively toured Europe.

Acknowledgements

I'd like to thank my supervisor and music editor Adrian Hull for checking scores and offering advice during the making of this book and Jacqui Gee my mother and editor for willingly checking over many edits.

Thanks to Luke Bocchetta for the great job writing the drum tracks and Becca Brown for her patience with all the photography.

Advanced Bass Tuition

A collection of exercises in advanced and solo techniques for bass guitar and a collection of study pieces which include these techniques.

The exercises and pieces are aimed to inspire creativity in the student's own compositions and approach to playing the bass guitar.

The book contains pictures, tablature, standard notation and explanations to help with the learning and development of these techniques.

A Cd is included with audio demonstrations of many exercises and drum accompaniments for the study pieces.

Printed in Great Britain
by Amazon